SWAN HUNTER

THE PRIDE AND THE TEARS

'Our forefathers built ships of oak; we build of iron.'
John Wigham Richardson, c.1865

Ian Rae and Ken Smith

Tyne Bridge Publishing

Acknowledgements:

The authors wish to thank the following people for their kind help in the preparation of this book: Swan Hunter (Tyneside) Ltd, Dick Gonsalez, Eddie Jackson, Norman Gilchrist, Johnny Miller, Brian Newman, Ian Buxton, Eric Hollerton, Stan Gamester, Tony Parker, David Mackenzie, Michael Irwin, Ged Henderson, Dick Keys, Norman Atkinson, Bob Koch, Bill Todd, Frank Gray, Bobby Sisterson, Carol Lawcock, Les Hodgson, Edith Corby, David Wood, Tyne and Wear Archives and the staff of Newcastle City Library.

Newcastle Libraries & Information Service gratefully acknowledge Swan Hunter (Tyneside) Ltd., for sponsorship of this book.

Photographs are copyright of the Swan Hunter Archive care of Tyne & Wear Archives unless otherwise indicated.

Published by
City of Newcastle upon Tyne
Newcastle Libraries & Information Service
Tyne Bridge Publishing, 2001, revised reprint 2008

ISBN: 9781857951066

Cataloguing-in-Publication Data: a catalogue record for this book is available from the British Library.

Printed by Statexcolourprint, Newcastle upon Tyne.

Front cover illustration:
Men (and one woman) stream up Swan's Bank c. early 1907. The *Mauretania* is in the background.

Back cover illustration:
Global Producer being prepared at Swan Hunter's Wallsend yard in early 2001 for North Sea floating production and storage duties in the Leadon Oilfield.

The illustration on the title page is from a brochure published by Swan, Hunter & Wigham Richardson Ltd and Associated Companies in 1929. The illustration on the contents page is from the *Tyneside Official Industrial Handbook*, c.1950.

Find other books by Ken Smith at www.tynebridgepublishing.co.uk

Books and free catalogue available from:

Tyne Bridge Publishing
Newcastle Libraries & Information Service
PO Box 88
Newcastle upon Tyne
NE99 1DX

Contents

Page

The Pride of Neptune — 5

A Talented Brother-in-Law — 9

To Capture the Riband — 13

Ships for the World — 17

Launched on the Tyne — 21

Floating and Dry — 25

A Family of Shipbuilders — 31

Creating the Ladies — 33

Life in the Yards — 35

Swan's at Play — 41

From Boom to Uncertainty — 44

The Time of Trouble — 49

A Phoenix from the Ashes — 52

Ships and their Stories — 56

MARINE ENGINEERS

SHIPBUILDERS

SWAN HUNTER & WIGHAM RICHARDSON LIMITED

•

WALLSEND & NEWCASTLE UPON TYNE

*The Spanish passenger- and troop-ship **Alfonso XII** under construction at the Neptune Shipyard, Low Walker, Newcastle, in c. late 1887. Men can be seen at work on the bow of the ship.*

The Pride of Neptune

The launch of the tiny paddle steamer *Victoria* into the River Tyne in 1860 at John Wigham Richardson's Neptune Yard began a business destined to merge in 1903 with C.S. Swan & Hunter to form one of the world's greatest shipbuilding companies.

The *Victoria* was the first vessel to be built by Wigham Richardson's newly established firm, whose Neptune Yard was situated at Low Walker, Newcastle. She was constructed to ferry passengers, cattle and horse-drawn vehicles across the Solent between Portsmouth and Ryde, Isle of Wight.

In setting up his business, Wigham Richardson had chosen a site which had formerly been the yard of John Coutts, a pioneer of iron shipbuilding on the Tyne. The riverside land was thus already laid out as a shipyard with three building berths.

After a few difficult early years, the yard began to prosper. Its workers and management turned out a wide variety of merchant vessels. However, John Wigham Richardson was a Quaker and his company did not seek orders for warships. That he was able to be so selective in his choice of work is an indication of the great demand for ships during the Victorian era.

In developing his business, Wigham Richardson was greatly assisted by a brilliant naval architect, Charles Denham Christie, who became a managing partner in the enterprise. Denham Christie was renowned for designing beautifully proportioned ships.

In 1902 the yard delivered its first cableship, the *Colonia*. During the next 80 or so years Neptune was to gain a worldwide reputation for construction of these specialised vessels, designed to lay and repair telephone or telegraph cables.

Other ships of significance built at the yard included the *Hornby Grange*, one of the world's first large, refrigerated cargo carriers. This mundane queen of the oceans left the Tyne for delivery to her owners in 1890. But perhaps the most illustrious vessel built at the yard in the 19th century was the Spanish passenger liner and troopship, the *Alfonso XII*, which was launched into the Tyne in March 1888.

John Wigham Richardson, founder of the Neptune Shipyard, Low Walker. A Quaker, Wigham Richardson would not undertake warship building, concentrating entirely on merchant vessels.

*The tiny paddle steamer **Victoria**, the first vessel to be built at the Neptune Yard (1860). She was launched as a ferry to carry passengers and livestock across the Solent between Portsmouth and the Isle of Wight.*

Yard workers must have felt great pride as the 408ft-long liner slid down the ways into the river. The launch ceremony was performed by the twin daughters of the ship's captain who cracked two bottles of champagne over the ship's bows, one on each side. John Wigham Richardson presented the girls with bouquets.

The daughters were among the guests sheltering from heavy rain under a tarpaulin canopy over the launch platform. Others were forced to rely on their hats, coats and umbrellas as they stood in the yard amid the downpour. These included hundreds of workers.

A group of 'ladies and gentlemen' had travelled down river to the yard from Newcastle Quayside in the Tyne General Ferry Company's steamer *Alice*, which had been specially chartered for the occasion. The heavy, slanting rain drove them below the open deck. When they reached Low Walker they joined other visitors on a tour of the yard's workshops prior to the launch. John Wigham Richardson himself conducted the tour. It was a welcome opportunity to get a little dry before the ceremony.

The *Newcastle Daily Journal* commented: 'When all had gathered it was really astonishing to discover how many had braved the storm in order to show respect for the genial and highly-esteemed head of the firm.'

The rain was the only disappointment of the day. 'The vessel, with slowly increasing speed, descended the ways with great steadiness, and was speedily pulled up. A more successful launch in this respect was perhaps never witnessed,' added the *Journal*. Afterwards, the guests toured the joiners' shop, before being given tea in the loft above the shop. Then the Newcastle party re-boarded the steamer *Alice* for the return trip to the Quayside.

At that date the *Alfonso XII* was the largest and most prestigious passenger ship ever launched on the Tyne. When completed, she was indeed an impressive vessel with her four prominent masts and two funnels, all sloped backwards (raked) thus giving an impression of speed and grace. Her long profile featured a clipper bow which added to her elegant appearance. Clipper bows were said at the time to be 'coming back into fashion'.

The ship's 'grand entrance' included an expensive marble staircase in the style of one at the Opera House in Paris, all compartments were lit by electric lighting and she was equipped with 2,000 cubic feet of refrigerated cargo space.

She had originally been designed for British owners as a cargo ship, which might carry a small number of passengers. However, while on

Alfonso XII, completed at the Neptune yard in 1888.

her building berth she was purchased by a Spanish company and converted into a major passenger liner, the vessel being intended to carry 800 troops or emigrants as well as 240 civilian passengers in first- and second-class cabins.

The change of plan was made possible by a Spanish government subsidy towards the ship's cost on condition that she would serve as a cruiser in time of war. The decks were arranged so that guns could be mounted if necessary. The ship was provided with a cellular double bottom. She was built for the Compania Transatlantica of Spain and operated mainly on the run between Cadiz and Havana in Cuba.

As well as constructing the ship, the Neptune Yard also built her triple expansion engines, linked to a single propeller, which gave her a service speed of around 15 to 16 knots. This was a fast speed in the 1880s. Running her trials off St Mary's

Island, Whitley Bay, the *Alfonso XII* clocked up slightly over 15 knots.

The vessel's boilers were also constructed at the yard. The Neptune engine and boiler works, set up in 1872, were managed by the able John Tweedy, who played a leading role in developing a system to reduce vibration in ships.

Not long before she was due to leave the Tyne for delivery to her Spanish owners, the *Alfonso XII* was moored at Jarrow Slake and thrown open to the public. Tickets to see the liner were one shilling each and the money raised was donated to Whitley Bay Convalescent Homes. The people of Tyneside were able to view a splendid example of the river's proud workmanship.

The *Alfonso XII* entered service in the autumn of 1888 and served as planned on the Spanish company's Cadiz-Havana service. Sometimes voyages were made between New York and Cuba and she also made trips to Manila in the Philippines. But after nearly 10 years of service she was lost during the Spanish-American War of 1898.

In July of that year the ship tried to enter Havana harbour in a bid to evade the US blockade of the island. However, she was spotted by an American armed patrol yacht, the USS *Hawk*, which chased her along the coastal waters of northern Cuba.

In her attempt to escape, the *Alfonso XII* tried to enter Port Mariel, west of Havana. She had easily outpaced the American vessel. Then disaster struck when she ran aground on rocks near the entrance to the port. Most of the ship's crew, passengers and troops are believed to have reached the shore safely in lifeboats. But American warships opened fire on the liner as she lay helpless on the reef, reducing her to a total wreck. It was a sad ending to the pride of the Neptune Yard.

Origins of the Swan Hunter business.

| 1853 Charles Mitchell founds **Low Walker Yard** | 1874 Charles Sheriton Swan Senior (brother-in-law of Charles Mitchell) takes over Wallsend Yard **C.S. Swan & Co.** | 1880 George Burton Hunter succeeds Charles Sheriton Swan as head of Wallsend Yard **C.S. Swan & Hunter & Co.** | 1903 Neptune and Wallsend Yards amalgamate **Swan, Hunter & Wigham Richardson Ltd.** |

1860
John Wigham Richardson founds
Neptune Yard

Newcastle Libraries

Swan Hunter's Wallsend shipyard c.1890.

A Talented Brother-in-Law

John Wigham Richardson was not the only shipbuilder to set up a business at Low Walker in the East End of Newcastle. Charles Mitchell, from Aberdeen, had established his own yard there in 1853. Romance blossomed for Charles when he met Anne Swan, the daughter of a farmer at Walker, and they were married at the new Walker Parish Church in 1854.

In 1873 Charles Mitchell stepped in to take over the running of another shipyard, this time at Wallsend, which had been managed by two of his business associates, Coulson and Cook, but which had hit financial difficulties. The following year Charles appointed his brother-in-law, Charles Sheriton Swan senior, as manager of this yard.

The resulting new business became known as C.S. Swan and Company. Swan's Wallsend Shipyard was born. Within a few years Charles Sheriton Swan had made a success of the business, recouping the losses of the previous firm. Mitchell must have been delighted with his talented brother-in-law.

But tragedy struck in 1879 when the hard-working Swan was killed in an accident in the English Channel. He was returning from a business trip to Russia with his wife when he fell from the bows of a paddle steamer, suffering fatal injuries when he was hit by one of the paddles. Charles had been looking at the then relatively new feathered-style paddles to see how they worked.

The vacuum left at the Wallsend Yard by the pioneering manager's death was filled by George Burton Hunter, a shipbuilder from Sunderland, who became the new managing director after entering into business partnership with Charles Sheriton Swan's widow, Mary. The firm was renamed C.S. Swan and Hunter in 1880. Charles and Mary's son, Charles Sheriton Swan junior, became a director at the age of 25 in 1895 when the business was turned into a limited company.

The role of George Burton Hunter in building up the reputation of Swan's for superbly designed and soundly

George Burton Hunter, who was Swan's chairman from 1895 to 1928. A tireless worker, his role in building up the company cannot be underestimated.

9

Andrew Laing, general manager of the Wallsend Slipway and Engineering Company. He led the company to become a world renowned builder of marine engines. Laing and his team designed the turbine engines for the **Mauretania**, *based upon principles developed by Sir Charles Parsons.*

constructed ships cannot be underestimated. Heading the business from 1880, he remained at the helm until his retirement as chairman in 1928 at the age of 81. A teetotaller, he was a passionate advocate of temperance. Possessing a strong Christian faith, he took an active interest in the welfare of the people of Wallsend and of those who worked at the yards, contributing large sums to charities and helping to provide for the disabled and poor.

Hunter was said to have devoted his whole life to work, putting in long hours from early morning to late in the evening to ensure the success of the business. A man of great energy, he seems to have been undaunted by obstacles. *The Shipyard*

magazine declared that his slogans were 'work; concentration and application to the job in hand; success is the result of persistent hard work, and failure is the inspiration for further work and bigger ideals'. He was knighted in 1918 for his services as head of Swan's during the First World War.

A milestone in the history of Tyne shipbuilding was reached in 1903 when C.S. Swan and Hunter merged with Wigham Richardson's company to form a new shipbuilding business. The Wallsend and Neptune yards were now united in what was to prove a highly successful partnership on the northern bank of the river. One of the main reasons for the amalgamation of the two companies was to combine their resources to bid for the prestigious *Mauretania* contract.

In the same year the new company, now known as Swan, Hunter and Wigham Richardson Ltd, took over The Tyne Pontoons and Dry Docks Company, which specialised in shiprepair and overhaul. The yard of this firm was situated between the Wallsend and Neptune yards. It became Swan's dry docks department.

Also in 1903, Swan, Hunter and Wigham Richardson acquired a controlling interest in the Wallsend Slipway and Engineering Company, whose works were situated a little to the east of the Wallsend yard close to Willington Quay. This company, originally formed to repair and refit ships, was by the early 1900s increasingly specialising in the production of marine engines and boilers under the able management of Andrew Laing, from Edinburgh. Eventually the slipways upon which vessels were repaired were dismantled and the company concentrated almost entirely upon engineering.

The early years of the 20th century saw other important developments in Swan's history. In 1912 it took over the Clydeside shipbuilder Barclay, Curle & Co Ltd., of Glasgow, and a shipbuilding business in Londonderry, Northern Ireland. In association with Philips of Dartmouth, Swan's also reopened a shipyard at Southwick, Sunderland, for the construction of moderately-sized vessels.

Meanwhile, Wallsend Slipway and Engineering was going

*The **Carpathia**, the ship which rescued the **Titanic** survivors in April 1912. Completed by C.S. Swan and Hunter at the Wallsend Yard in 1903, she was driven by quadruple expansion engines built by the Wallsend Slipway and Engineering Company Ltd., directed by Andrew Laing.*

from strength to strength under the management of Andrew Laing. He became general manager of this company in 1896 and was soon reorganising and enlarging the works so that it could provide engines and boilers for the largest vessels, including passenger liners and major warships. One of his first important contracts was to build the machinery for the Russian icebreaker *Yermak*, which was launched at Charles Mitchell's Low Walker Yard.

This brilliant engineer was a pioneer in the use of oil fuel for ships, continuing the work of his predecessor at the company, William Boyd. Laing developed a successful system to enable oil to be used efficiently for marine boilers.

Under his guidance Wallsend Slipway and Engineering gained a reputation for soundly constructed quadruple expansion engines, providing them for the Swan's-built Cunard liners *Ivernia* and *Carpathia*. In addition, Laing was also one of the earliest builders of marine steam turbines. Battleships such as HMS *Queen Elizabeth*, and the Tyne-built HMS *Malaya*, HMS *Superb* and HMS *Nelson* all received their turbine engines from the company.

Commenting on Laing's achievements after his death in 1931, *The Shipyard* magazine, Swan's house journal, said: 'One of Mr Laing's chief characteristics was the confidence he inspired in his staff, in his workmen, and in the minds of those who entrusted him with important work This last was exemplified by the sending of the battleship *Queen Elizabeth* straight into action without sea trials. He was one of the great marine engine builders of his day.'

It was Andrew Laing who led the team at Wallsend Slipway and Engineering which constructed the powerful turbine engines for the *Mauretania*, the greatest passenger liner ever launched on the Tyne. She was to prove Swan, Hunter and Wigham Richardson's most celebrated achievement.

*A stern view of the **Mauretania** on the stocks in her building shed before her launch at the Wallsend Yard in 1906. Two of the four giant propellers are visible. The huge vessel dwarfs a group of workers, bottom right.*

To Capture the Riband

The great passenger liner *Mauretania* was the pride of the Tyne. Built by Swan Hunter and Wigham Richardson, she was a ship of exceptional quality and outstanding performance. The vessel was the largest and most magnificent passenger ship launched on the river. She served as a floating luxury hotel, troopship, hospital ship and cruise liner during a glittering careering lasting 28 years. Above all, she was a speed queen, holding the Blue Riband for the fastest crossing of the North Atlantic longer than any other liner.

Even today, the name *Mauretania* is a symbol of the Tyne's fine workmanship and spirited endeavour. She, more than any other vessel, established the river's reputation as a shipbuilding centre which could turn out vessels of the highest standard. She was indeed the crowning glory of Swan's.

The building of the liner took place against a background of Anglo-German rivalry upon the oceans. In the opening years of the 20th century German passenger liners had been the fastest on the North Atlantic and most could easily be converted into armed auxiliary cruisers should war break out.

Britain's Cunard company was worried by the German challenge and eventually persuaded the British government of the day to advance a £2.6 million loan towards the construction of two fast passenger ships.

The government agreed to the loan and to the granting of an annual subsidy towards the upkeep of the vessels on condition that they would if necessary serve as armed cruisers in wartime. It was also stipulated that Cunard should remain a British company and the ships were expected to achieve between 24 and 25 knots in moderate weather. One ship would become *Mauretania*, the other *Lusitania*.

Mauretania was launched at Swan's Wallsend Shipyard on September 20 1906 by the Dowager Duchess of Roxburghe. The event was watched by thousands of spectators on both sides of the river.

Afterwards, the vessel was towed by tugs to her fitting-out quay and over the next year she was provided with her lavish woodwork cabins and public rooms, engines and funnels. The huge turbine engines and boilers were lifted into the vessel by the floating crane *Titan*.

By October 1907 the giant ship was ready to depart the river for delivery to her owners, the Cunard Line, in Liverpool and for her official trials in the Irish Sea and Firth of Clyde. The building of the liner had been an outstanding achievement by the workers and management of the Wallsend Yard.

Mauretania left the Tyne on her delivery voyage on October 22 1907. Tens of thousands of people crowded the river's banks all the way from the Wallsend Yard to Tynemouth and South Shields, cheering the magnificent ship as she passed gracefully on her way to the sea with an escort of tugs. The liner was also saluted by the buzzers of shipyards and engine works and the sirens of ocean-going vessels and small craft.

The 31,938 gross tons *Mauretania* was 790ft long overall with a maximum beam of 88ft. She was driven by powerful turbine engines, built by Wallsend Slipway and Engineering. The engines were constructed to the designs of Andrew Laing and his team and based upon principles developed by Tyneside inventor Sir Charles Parsons. Wallsend Slipway and Engineering also constructed the ship's boilers. The engines were linked to four huge propellers, each initially fitted with three blades. In addition, the liner featured four impressive

*Workers stream up Swan's Bank, Wallsend, at the end of the day shift in c. early 1907. The four funnels of the **Mauretania**, then being fitted out, dominate the background. One woman (in hat, centre) can be seen among the countless men hurrying up the bank.*

funnels bearing the traditional Cunard red and black colours.

Mauretania departed on her maiden voyage from Liverpool to New York on November 16 1907, but a storm prevented her from capturing the coveted Blue Riband for the westward passage. However, on her return voyage to Britain she broke the eastward record with a speed of 23.69 knots and held on to this honour for the next 22 years.

In May 1908 the liner broke the westward record, at last capturing the Riband for both directions. In doing so, she had beaten her Clyde-built sister *Lusitania*. A friendly duel developed between the two vessels and in July 1908 *Lusitania* regained the westward honour. But finally, in September 1909, *Mauretania* again achieved a record speed westwards, holding on to this accolade for 20 years. On this famous 1909 crossing she achieved an average speed of 26.06 knots.

By this time her four propellers had each been fitted with four blades, instead of three, and this had improved her rate of knots.

During the First World War, the Tyne's most famous passenger ship carried troops and also served as a floating hospital. In the summer of 1915 she made three voyages to the Aegean Sea, taking soldiers to the ill-fated Gallipoli campaign. Later that year she was converted into a hospital ship and returned to the Aegean three more times, on these occasions transporting men wounded at Gallipoli home to Britain.

In 1918 *Mauretania* was again used as a troopship and temporarily renamed HMS *Tuber Rose*. She carried thousands of American soldiers from New York to Liverpool on their way to join the Allied armies on the Western Front. After the war, the liner carried many of those who had survived the conflict back to the United States.

With her trooping duties done the ship returned to civilian service with Cunard. Her home port was switched from Liverpool to Southampton, although her destination in North America remained New York.

In 1921 she steamed back to Swan's Wallsend Yard where she was converted from a coal to an oil-burning ship. In addi-

Mauretania returns to the Tyne to be converted from a coal to an oil-burning ship in late 1921. Crowds line the banks to welcome her 'home'.

tion, improvements were carried out to her passenger accommodation. Her oil conversion improved her performance.

For the next eight years she successfully plied the Southampton-New York route and became affectionately know as the 'Grand Old Lady of the Atlantic.' In 1927 she steamed 77,500 miles at an average speed of 25.5 knots. The legendary ship did not lose the Blue Riband until 1929, when it was wrested from her by the more powerfully engined German liner *Bremen*.

During her final years *Mauretania* was used extensively as a cruise ship, sailing mostly to the West Indies and the Mediterranean. Her hull was painted white.

*Tribute to the river. **Mauretania** stops off the mouth of the Tyne in July 1935 to pay a tribute to her Tyneside origins. She was on her way to the breaker's yard near Rosyth. Many small craft came out from the river to greet her and the ship fired rockets in a salute to the Tyne.*

At last, in 1935, after a career unequalled in maritime history, she sailed for the breaker's yard near Rosyth on the Firth of Forth. But on her way northwards she stopped at the mouth of the Tyne as a tribute to her North-East origins.

Thousands of people lined every vantage point along the seafronts between Whitley Bay and South Shields and they were rewarded with a sight never to be forgotten. The liner came to a halt two miles off the Tyne piers and fired rockets from her bridge as a further mark of admiration for the workmanship of the Tyne. It was a salute in particular to the men of Swan's Wallsend Yard and of Wallsend Slipway and Engineering.

There were tears in people's eyes along the seafronts as the legendary ship moved away northwards towards Scotland on the final leg of her final voyage.

Mauretania's last master, Captain A.T. Brown, sent a wireless message to the Lord Mayor of Newcastle. It read: 'Thank you for your greeting. For 28 years I have striven to be a credit to you and now my day is done. Though I pass on, may Tyneside ever reach out to further and greater triumphs. With pride and affection I greet you. Farewell – *Mauretania*.'

It was a moving tribute to the river where she had first started out on her highly successful life.

Ships for the World

Today, a new company, Swan Hunter (Tyneside) Ltd., is leading a revival of shipbuilding on the Tyne. It is following in the footsteps of one of the world's greatest producers of ocean queens. During more than 130 years of operation the old Swan Hunter company built over 1,600 ships at the Wallsend and Neptune yards.

Almost every type of vessel was launched, including passenger liners, cargo liners, cargo-passenger liners, passenger ferries, train ferries, oil tankers, ice-breakers, cableships, Great Lake freighters, cruisers, frigates, destroyers, sloops, Royal Fleet Auxiliary ships and steam yachts. The output even included a battleship, HMS *Anson*, built during the Second World War.

Swan's reputation for well-built ships was the result of pride in doing a good job, determination to overcome problems, hard work, skilled craftsmanship and a readiness to adopt innovations. Swan Hunter thus achieved a high place in the league of the world's top shipbuilders.

The company had many customers, with orders being received from countries throughout the globe, including Britain, France, Portugal, Spain, Italy, Sweden, Canada, Norway, China and Japan. They came to the Tyne because of the river's reputation for well-built vessels, created by men of energy, skill and pride in their work.

During those 130 years at the Wallsend and Neptune yards shipbuilding changed greatly. In the late 1880s and the 1890s steel superseded iron as the material for building hulls. The main advantages of steel over iron are its greater strength combined with less thickness, resulting in less weight.

The **Peter G. Campbell**, Swan's first all-welded vessel, on her berth at the Wallsend Yard. She was launched in 1933 and was also the first all-welded vessel built on the Tyne.

In addition, the skilled but arduous task of hand-riveting was replaced by pneumatic and hydraulic riveting machines. In turn, these were gradually replaced by welding, an important advance which Swan Hunter helped to pioneer. By the 1930s welding for the smaller thicknesses of steel was becoming common.

Swan's first all-welded ship was the 179ft-long barge *Peter G. Campbell,* built for carrying oil in bulk on the Great Lakes and canals of Canada. Ordered by Dominion Tankers Ltd., of Toronto, the *Peter G. Campbell* was launched at the Wallsend Yard in 1933.

This rivetless vessel was electrically welded throughout, resulting in a lighter ship with consequently greater carrying capacity. As well as being a 'first' for Swan's, she was also the first all-welded ship built on the Tyne. Designed to be towed, she contained no propelling machinery. The *Peter G. Campbell* was delivered across the Atlantic to Montreal by tug.

Rivets thus gradually gave way to welding and other changes took place in the wake of this development. By the 1970s ships were no longer being built plate-by-plate on the Tyne slipways. Instead they were welded together in prefabricated sections in workshops which were then joined up on the slipways like a giant jigsaw puzzle.

Besides welding, the design and construction of oil tankers was another field in which Swan Hunter was an important pioneer. These ships included eight supertankers of around 250,000 deadweight tonnes built at the Wallsend Yard between 1968 and 1976.

The company was a leader in tanker design until the mid 1970s, completing 46 vessels for the British Tanker Co and 41 for Shell. Other customers included the Eagle Oil and Burmah Oil companies. These ships contributed greatly to the prosperity of the company.

Cargo and cargo-passenger liners were also a mainstay of the order books, with 30 being delivered for the British India Steam Navigation Company, 24 for the Ellerman Line and 22 for the Port Line. Orders for passenger liners came from such companies as the prestigious Cunard Line, the Norwegian-America Line, Shaw, Savill and Albion Line and France's SGTM Line.

Swan's received orders for some of the most prestigious passenger liners, the success of *Mauretania* greatly enhancing the company's reputation in this field. These vessels included *Dominion Monarch*, which was the largest motor-driven passenger ship in the world when completed at Wallsend in 1939. She also had a large cargo-carrying capacity. The *Dominion Monarch* was built for Shaw,

The launch party for the passenger liner **Dominion Monarch** *at Wallsend on July 27 1938. Pictured on the extreme right is Charles Sheriton Swan junior. Next to him is Lady Essendon, wife of the chairman of Shaw, Savill & Albion Line, who performed the launch ceremony.*

The **Titan II** floating crane alongside the passenger liner **Dominion Monarch** in 1938. The ship is being fitted out at the Wallsend jetty following her launch.

*The icebreaker **Dobrina Nikitich**. She was one of four icebreakers launched for Russia by Swan's in 1916.*

Savill and Albion Line's London-New Zealand service and served as a troopship during the Second World War.

Highly specialised ships were also a feature of the yards. Among those launched in the early 20th century were four icebreakers for Tsarist Russia, built in 1916, a year before the outbreak of revolution. Russian crew members were stationed in the yards, standing by as the vessels neared completion to learn how to operate them.

At this date, temporary lighting used to illuminate darkened compartments aboard ships under construction consisted of candles. Electric lights had yet to arrive in this field of shipbuilding. After several weeks, the stores management in one of the yards noticed that a large number of candles had disappeared. After investigating, they established that the workmen were not taking them home. Instead, the poorly nourished Russian crews were eating them. The candles were made from tallow.

Three of the Swan's icebreakers were built at Neptune, the *Ilia Muromets*, *Dobrina Nikitich* and *Kosa Minin*. The fourth ship, the *Kniaz Pojarsky*, was built at Wallsend. *Dobrina Nikitich* was based in Vladivostock in Russia's Far East. For many years there was a superb builder's model of this vessel in the main entrance hall to the Wallsend Yard. It served as a reminder of Swan's connection with Russia's frozen seas.

Launched on the Tyne

Three launches which took place between the world wars illustrate the varied and international nature of Swan's customers.

In 1932 Swan's launched the train ferry *Changkiang* for service on the Yangtse River in China between Pukow and Nanking. The ship, built at Neptune, provided an important link in the country's rail network, bringing together the Beijing-Pukow railway to the north of the Yangtse and the Nanking-Shanghai railway to the south. The 372ft-long vessel, with a maximum beam of 58.5ft, was capable of taking three trains on three lines of track. Her hull was divided into watertight bulkheads extending to the height of the upper deck.

The launch took place on October 12 1932, the ceremony being performed by Madame Quo Tai-Chi, wife of the Chinese Ambassador to Britain. She was accompanied by officials from the Chinese Legation in London.

The party on the launch platform formally acknowledged the Chinese Republic by saluting the country's flag. This involved turning towards the flag and bowing three times. Madame Quo then named the ship *Changkiang* (Long River, the popular name for the Yangtse) and broke a bottle of wine over the ship's bows. After the launch the guests were given lunch at Swan's Staff Institute.

Changkiang sailed out to China from the mouth of the Tyne under her own steam, a considerable feat for a vessel designed only for river work. During her crossing of the Mediterranean to reach the Suez Canal she came up against a fierce storm but survived the battering.

The train ferry entered service a year after her launch. The opening ceremony was performed by a Chinese girl swimmer,

*The **Changkiang** enters the Tyne at the Neptune Yard, October 12 1932.*

The launch party for the Chinese train ferry **Changkiang** in October 1932. Madame Quo Tai-Chi, the lady on the left, wife of the Chinese Ambassador to Britain, performed the ceremony at the Neptune Yard. Sir G.B. Hunter is far left.

was originally laid down as a British ship, HMS *Phaeton*, but later transferred to the Australian navy while still on her building berth and renamed after the famous Australian city.

The cruiser was launched on September 22 1934, the ceremony being performed by Mrs Bruce, wife of the High Commissioner for Australia, Stanley Melbourne Bruce. Also present was the then chairman of Swan's, John Denham Christie, son of Neptune's pioneering ship designer, Charles Denham Christie.

The singing of the usual naval hymn *Eternal Father Strong to Save* was accompanied by the Swan's works band, a traditional feature of most launches. A large detachment of ratings from the Tyne's Royal Naval Reserve ship, HMS *Calliope*, was drawn up at the bow of the cruiser.

Mrs Bruce then named the ship *Sydney*, released the triggers holding the launchways and as the vessel began to move broke a bottle of Australian wine on her bow.

After the ceremony guests were given tea in one of the platers' sheds which had been decorated with flags and flowers. Mrs Bruce was presented with a souvenir of the launch, a silver bowl designed by Reid & Sons of Newcastle and decorated with the head of the river god Tyne in bold relief.

Displacing 7,000 tons, *Sydney* was equipped with geared turbine engines and watertube boilers built by Wallsend Slipway & Engineering. The engines were linked to four propellers. She ran successful trials off the mouth of the Tyne and on the measured mile at St Abb's Head, Berwickshire, before hand-over in late 1935.

But fate was to prove no kinder to this ship than it had been to the *Changkiang*. Tragically, the *Sydney* was lost with all her

Yang Hsiu-Ching, who had won honours at a sports meeting in Nanking. Miss Yang cut ribbons stretched across the approach bridge to the ferry and was then presented with a basket of flowers and a silver trophy.

Changkiang provided an excellent service for the railway link but fate was not to be kind to her. She was lost during the Second World War when she was sunk by the Chinese to prevent her capture by the invading Japanese forces.

China was one far flung destination for an order. Another was Down Under. The Australian cruiser HMAS *Sydney* was launched in 1934 at the Wallsend Yard. The two-funnel *Sydney*

crew of over 600 men after a battle with the German raider ship *Comorin* off Shark Bay, Western Australia, in November 1941.

Comorin, a disguised merchant ship which had been converted into an armed auxiliary cruiser, was sunk by the *Sydney's* powerful guns, but not before the *Comorin* had succeeded in torpedoing her opponent.

The result was that fire broke out aboard the *Sydney* and she was last seen by the Germans moving away at slow speed, in flames. It is believed the blaze may have reached a magazine and that she blew up before sinking. Neither she nor her crew of 645 were ever seen again. The loss of the *Sydney* was one of the worst disasters to befall the Australian navy.

The *Changkiang* and the *Sydney* had been unlucky, but many other ships built by the company enjoyed much longer careers. In early 1929 the company launched two passenger ferries for the Swedish Lloyd Line's London-Gothenburg service. The first of these ships to enter the Tyne was the *Suecia*. She was launched in January at the Wallsend Yard. No problems of any significance were encountered.

However, her sister ship, the *Britannia*, was hit by the bitterly cold weather which gripped the Tyne barely a month later. She was awaiting her launch on February 26 at the Neptune

Wallsend cruiser. The launch of the Australian cruiser HMAS **Sydney** *at Wallsend on September 22 1934.*

Frozen to the slipway. The strain can be seen on the faces of the launch party for the Swedish Lloyd Line's ferry **Britannia** *at Neptune in February 1929. Bitterly cold weather had frozen the ship to the ways and she refused to move.*

The Swedish Lloyd Line ran ships between London and Gothenberg. The company's **Britannia** *and sister ship* **Suecia** *(seen here) were both built by Swan Hunter and Wigham Richardson.*

Yard when it was discovered the grease on the ways had frozen hard. The *Britannia* refused to move. The ship was frozen to the slipway.

The managing director of Swedish Lloyd and his wife had journeyed from Sweden with friends for the launch day and they were naturally disappointed when all that could be done was to name the ship. They were scheduled to stay in the North-East for only one more day.

Swan's therefore decided that a special effort must be made to launch the *Britannia* on their last day. Accordingly, a team of shipwrights, led by their foreman Mr Sambidge, worked tirelessly all night on the slipway. They removed two thirds of the sliding ways, scraped the frozen grease off them, re-greased the ways and then relaid them.

Steam pipes were fitted between the ways, the steam being supplied from the boiler of a locomotive which was brought up alongside the ship. Coke fires were also lit to keep the berth as warm as possible. All was now ready and fingers were crossed.

The efforts of these hardy workmen were to prove successful. At 5pm on February 27 the Swedish party were delighted to see the *Britannia* slide into the Tyne without any problems. The launch was a triumph for the team of shipwrights in the face of extremely cold and difficult conditions.

The *Britannia* and *Suecia* went on to have successful lives lasting over 40 years.

Floating and Dry

In 1931 Swan's completed a floating dock which was towed 14,000 nautical miles from Wallsend to Wellington, New Zealand, by Dutch tugs. It remains one of the longest tows on record and was an extraordinary feat of determination and seamanship.

Known as the Jubilee Floating Dock, she was launched at Wallsend in three sections which were then bolted together and riveted. The dock was intended for the repair of ships at Wellington Harbour and had a lifting capacity of up to 17,000 tons.

The last section was launched into the Tyne on June 3 1931 and six days later a test was carried out. This involved the dock being sunk into the river as far as the depth of the water alongside the jetty would allow. She was kept at that depth for half an hour to prove that the main deck and bulkheads were tight. The dock was then pumped dry and prepared for the epic voyage to New Zealand.

On July 15 she departed the Wallsend Shipyard under the tow of a pair of powerful steam tugs, the *Zwarte Zee* and the *Roode Zee*, owned by L. Smit & Company's International Sleepdienst, of Rotterdam, an organisation famed for its great experience in towing work. The Dutch vessels, which were positioned ahead, were assisted by three Tyne tugs astern, which stayed with the dock until the mouth of the river was reached.

From then on, the Dutch tugs were on their own. The floating dock made good progress down the East Coast, averaging nearly 100 miles a day. In the English Channel the *Roode Zee* was replaced by another steam tug, the *Witte Zee*.

The dock passed Gibraltar on July 30 and reached Port Said at the head of the Suez Canal on August 18. It took the dock only 36 hours to pass through the canal. Aden was reached on September 7. The voyage was progressing ahead of schedule.

Crossing the Indian Ocean, the dock was towed through the Torres Strait between Queensland in Australia and New Guinea. Stormy conditions were encountered in the Tasman Sea

Epic voyage of 1931. The Jubilee Floating Dock is towed into Wellington Harbour, New Zealand, by Dutch tugs after a voyage of 14,000 nautical miles. The marathon tow from Wallsend had taken a little over five months.

between Australia and New Zealand, but on December 28 1931 the *Zwarte Zee* and *Witte Zee* brought the dock safely into Wellington Harbour after a voyage, allowing for deviations from the straight course, of about 14,000 nautical miles.

The journey had taken a little over five months. Indeed, the floating dock had arrived at its destination early. It had not been expected to reach New Zealand until the beginning of February 1932. The tow reflected great credit on the Dutch tugs and their crews.

By this date floating docks had become one of Swan's specialities. The company built 36 for owners worldwide, including a giant one for Singapore, launched in 1927 for the British Admiralty and delivered to her destination in two parts, comprising seven sections.

The last sections, again towed by L. Smit tugs, reached the Naval Base at Singapore in October 1928. The dock was used for the repair of British warships in the Far East. Her lifting capacity was 55,000 tons. In total area the floor of this dock was said to be so spacious that it could easily contain two football pitches as large as Newcastle United's ground.

Floating docks were also built for Cuba, Peru, Japan, Russia, Nigeria, Bermuda, Holland, Aden, Trinidad and South Africa. Among the earliest was the Havana Dock, Cuba, launched in 1897 for the Spanish government.

Bound for the Far East. A section of the Singapore Dock, built for the Admiralty, is towed from the mouth of the Tyne by tugs in 1928 at the beginning of its delivery voyage to the Far East.

*The cruiser HMS **Nottingham** in the No. 2 Dry Dock at Wallsend in September 1914. The crew of the four-funnelled ship can be seen on deck.*

*Heavy lifter. The **Titan II** floating crane lifting a gate for a new dry dock at Wallsend in 1934.*

But although these water-borne docks were one of Swan's many success stories, its own dry docks department, situated between the Wallsend and Neptune yards, carried out maintenance, overhaul and repairs to countless ships. The work may have lacked the prestigious image of shipbuilding, but the repair of vessels was vital to the world's trade and provided bread-and-butter employment for the Tyne's hard-working men.

Throughout much of the 20th century Swan's Wallsend Dry Docks (also known as 'graving' docks) were kept busy overhauling ships of many descriptions, including oil tankers, cargo liners and Royal Fleet Auxiliary vessels. By late 1934 the department had three dry docks, the last of these, and also the longest and widest at that date, being completed earlier that year. The steel gates for this dock were built at the Wallsend Yard and lifted into position by the floating crane *Titan II*.

The first Titan crane had been ordered from Germany specifically to help with the *Mauretania* contract, arriving on the river in 1906. This heavy-lift floating crane was wrecked in December 1921 when a westerly gale caused her to break loose from her moorings at Hebburn and she was swept down river, colliding with several ships. The wreck of the *Titan* was eventually towed out into the North Sea and sunk.

The Dutch-built *Titan II* was bought by Swan's as a replacement and made her appearance in the Tyne in 1922. Swan's formed a company with Wallsend Slipway and Engineering and Hawthorn Leslie to operate the crane and hire it out for work up and down the river. This second crane was fitted to a new barge in c.1979 and renamed *Titan III*. The name is perhaps a little misleading since there have been three barges but only two Titan cranes. *Titan III* is still based at the Wallsend Shipyard.

The third dry dock at Swan's was not to be the last. A fourth, even larger one was built in the 1960s.

With its proud workforce, well-equipped yards, dry docks and wealth of experience the company proved itself of great value to Britain throughout both world wars.

During the First World War, Swan's built 55 ships for the Admiralty. The list is impressive: two cruisers, 28 torpedo boat destroyers, a monitor (heavy gun ship), five submarines, seven sloops, two Q-ships (armed vessels disguised as peaceful merchant ships), seven convoy sloops, one troopship, one repair and depot ship and one hospital ship. Ordinary merchant vessels, totalling over 290,588 gross tons, were also constructed.

The dry docks repaired 556 vessels during the conflict, 249 of which were warships. They included 41 light cruisers, 74 torpedo boat destroyers and 72 submarines. Swan's also carried out repairs to the battlecruiser HMS *Lion*, famed for her role at

Jutland in 1916 as the flagship of Rear Admiral Sir David Beatty. The Swan's-built cruiser HMS *Comus* and several of its destroyers also fought at Jutland.

In 1912 the company had completed a floating dock for the Royal Navy. She was capable of accommodating battleships and had a lifting capacity of 33,000 tons. The dock was based at Sheerness until 1915 and was then towed back to the Tyne, where she was moored at Jarrow Slake and used for the repair of ships throughout the rest of the First World War. She did not leave the Tyne until 1923.

In addition to its maritime contribution to the war effort, the com-

*Jutland fighter. The cruiser HMS **Comus** alongside the Wallsend Shipyard in May 1915. The **Comus** fought at the Battle of Jutland a year later, and survived the conflict. A 'wave' is painted on her bow, a device to confuse the enemy by making her seem to be travelling faster than she might actually be.*

pany set up a shell-making workshop which employed mainly women workers. Over 270,000 six-inch shells were forged and nearly 100,000 of them completed, ready for filling.

During the Second World War, Swan's again made a very important contribution. The combined output of Wallsend and Neptune included a battleship, two fleet aircraft carriers, four escort aircraft carriers, five cruisers, 29 destroyers, eight frigates and one minesweeper. In addition, 25 landing craft were built. The dry docks were also kept busy with numerous repairs to damaged vessels.

A typical example of repair work was the destroyer HMS *Achates*, which was towed to the dry docks after her bows were severely damaged when she was mined off Iceland in July 1941. Work on repairing the ship was completed in April the following year.

In the summer of 1940 Swan's completed a floating dock for the Royal Navy to be used at Scapa Flow in the Orkneys for the repair of warships damaged during convoys. Lieutenant Commander Michael Irwin (RNVR, retired), of Gosforth, Newcastle, was a young sub-lieutenant serving in the sloop

*Workers and guests pack the Wallsend shipyard for the launch of the cruiser HMS **Edinburgh** on March 31 1938.*

Two merchant ships in the convoy were sunk.

'I am sure that the attack was meant for the floating dock, but they were a day late,' adds Michael.

Warships from Swan's which served with distinction during the Second World War included the cruiser HMS *Edinburgh*, completed at the Wallsend Yard in 1939. The vessel took part in the hunt for the German battleship *Bismark*. However, *Edinburgh* was sunk with a cargo of Russian gold bullion during the Russian Arctic convoys in 1942. The gallant ship was hit by torpedoes from a U-boat and badly damaged. There were many casualties.

But the Tyne cruiser continued to fire one or two of her last operational guns when later attacked by a flotilla of German destroyers. Being badly damaged and unable to return to base, she was deliberately sunk by one of her own escorts after the survivors had been evacuated.

Other vessels from Swan's which put in sterling service included the cruiser HMS *Coventry* and the Tribal Class destroyer HMS *Tartar*, which in 1942 was part of the convoy escort sent to relieve the siege of Malta. The Colony Class cruisers HMS *Newfoundland*, HMS *Gambia* and HMS *Mauritius* were also from the slipways of the company. Wallsend's only battleship, HMS *Anson*, provided cover for the Russian Arctic convoys. When the war ended in 1945, Swan, Hunter & Wigham Richardson had once again shown itself to be a precious asset to Britain.

HMS *Lowestoft* which visited the Tyne with her sister ship, HMS *Egret*, to escort the dock, towed by tugs, to Scapa. The slow journey northwards passed without incident.

'We took the dock northwards at only four or five knots, because of the tugs, and were extremely lucky to reach Scapa Flow unscathed,' says Michael.

However, a day after the dock was safely delivered, the *Lowestoft* was leading the escort of a convoy southwards from Scapa when it was attacked by German aircraft in the Moray Firth. Sub-Lieutenant Irwin was guiding the *Lowestoft*'s guns which shot down a Heinkel flying in low for a torpedo attack.

A Family of Shipbuilders

David Swan, of Newcastle, the great grandson of Charles Sheriton Swan senior, represented the fourth generation of his family to be associated with the company. David worked at Swan's for 26 years as an engineer in the quality control department.

His grandfather, Charles Sheriton Swan junior, was chairman of the business during the Second World War and was knighted for his services to the war effort. David says that Charles had been reluctant to accept the honour at first and did so only on the proviso that he was accepting the knighthood on behalf of all those who worked for the company. He thus acknowledged the immense contribution made by the entire workforce in building and repairing ships during the conflict.

David tells of how during the Depression in the early 1930s Charles junior kept men in employment at the shipyards even when orders were scarce or non-existent by setting them to work on making garden furniture. 'He did this because he did not want the workforce to be disbanded,' says David. 'He wanted to keep the men together so that they would be available as a skilled team when orders for ships did eventually come in. My grandfather knew the value of his workforce.'

David still has several small diaries kept by his grandfather which record, in meticulous but small handwriting, many of the ships launched. The entries detail facts and figures about each vessel, such as tonnage, dimensions, engines etc.

'He was totally dedicated to shipbuilding and had hardly any other interests outside his work,' adds David. 'He did, however, enjoy motor cars.'

Charles junior and his wife, Gertrude, had four children, one son and three daughters. Their son, Sheriton Clements Swan, was David's father. Sheriton eventually became a director of the firm. He had qualified as an ordinary architect rather than a naval architect and with his wife, Rosalind, designed interiors for several ships.

David joined Swan's in 1968 and was based at the Wallsend yard as a quality control engineer testing the machinery aboard ships. Among his most difficult jobs was to test the cargo handling equipment for a liquid gas tanker. He also tested

Charles Sheriton Swan junior, son of Swan's founder, who became a director of C.S. Swan and Hunter at the age of 25 and was knighted for his services to shipbuilding during the Second World War.

machinery on several of the supertankers built by Swan's, including the steam turbine driven cargo handling equipment for *Esso Northumbria*.

*Meticulous notebook. A page from one of Charles Sheriton Swan junior's notebooks giving facts and figures about the **Mauretania**.*

At first specialising in the merchant ship side of the business, he later joined the warship section and worked on the aircraft carriers *Illustrious* and *Ark Royal*, among Swan's most important contracts since the Second World War. On one occasion, on sea trials off Alnmouth, Northumberland, David found himself in charge of one of these aircraft carriers' engines at night. An easterly or north-easterly wind increased in strength and the anchor began dragging, probably because the seabed consisted of smoothly shelving rock. The huge ship began moving towards the shore. David received an urgent request from the bridge to start up the engines.

A technical problem prevented him from switching on the power for all the engines but he was able to start up one main engine shaft. It proved sufficient to swing the aircraft carrier away from the shore and out of any possible danger.

David Swan, great grandson of Swan's founder.

Creating the Ladies

After all the immense care and effort taken in building a ship it is hardly surprising that those involved become attached to the vessel they have created. It is 'their' ship, a lady of the sea which they have brought into being. Johnny Miller has this feeling about many of the vessels he worked on.

Johnny started work in the Neptune Yard as an apprentice draughtsman in 1948. Ten years later he transferred to Vickers Armstrongs' Walker Naval Yard, a short distance up river. He eventually became an assistant yard manager in charge of production. This meant he was responsible for managing the building and outfitting of ships.

Later, following the amalgamation of shipbuilding businesses on the Tyne and nationalisation, he returned to Swan's and was a manager at the Wallsend Yard, again in charge of building and outfitting. He worked on the *Ark Royal* and *Illustrious*.

Johnny recalls with pride and satisfaction being able to watch a ship take shape from the planning, through to keel laying, construction on the berth, launch, fitting out, sea trials and hand-over. In the earlier days of his career ships were still being built entirely on the slipways, plate-by-plate.

The construction of vessels in prefabricated sections in workshops before assembly on the slipways began to develop in a major way in the 1970s, although Johnny remembers that as early as 1958 a vessel was constructed in this way at the Walker Naval Yard.

Johnny was also a manager working on the building of the magnificent passenger liner *Vistafjord* at Neptune. Constructed for the Norwegian America Line, but now sailing with Cunard

Eddie Jackson, front right, with other drawing office apprentices pose with an anchor chain aboard a Swan's ship, the **Helix** *or the* **Helcion**, *in the 1950s. Front, left, is Fred Taylor, who became a technical director, and at the back are John Steele, left, later chief executive, and Don Olsen.*

as the *Caronia*, the *Vistafjord* was completed in 1973.

Johnny recalls sailing with the ship on her delivery voyage to Norway. He tells of the proud moment when she sailed up the Oslo Fjord to the Norwegian capital and was greeted with cascades of water from fireboats and hundreds of small motor craft.

He was responsible for overseeing the building of the container ship *Atlantic Conveyor* at the Walker Naval Yard. She was sunk during the Falklands War in 1982. 'It broke my heart,' he says. 'I thought: They've sunk my ship.' However, a second *Atlantic Conveyor* was built by Swan's to replace the first, this time at Wallsend. She was completed in 1985.

Among those who carried out the preparation work for this second *Atlantic Conveyor* was Eddie Jackson, of Tynemouth, who joined the drawing office at the Wallsend Yard in 1951. He eventually became a drawing office section leader and retired in 1986 after nearly 35 years with Swan's.

Eddie remembers helping to draw the 'lines' for the *Bergensfjord*, an elegant passenger ship built at Wallsend for the Norwegian America Line and launched in 1955 by Princess Astrid of Norway. He says: 'The Norwegians were good to work with. I found them to be fair and genuine. They recognised when you had difficulties and helped you to overcome them.'

Both Eddie and Johnny stress the special nature of building ships. 'What you are building is a small city in a self-contained package,' comments Johnny. Eddie adds: 'It's unique. A ship is a city in an envelope. Everything has to be designed and installed in a peculiarly restricted space. All the systems for living must fit into that space, including such things as water purification plant, plumbing, and electrical installations.'

One of Eddie's other early jobs was working on drawings for the destroyer HMS *Daring* in the early 1950s. Years later, while on holiday in Greece, he was surprised but delighted to learn that the ship had given assistance to the Greeks during an earthquake by delivering vital food and medical supplies.

'It made the hair stand up on the back of my neck to see a picture of the *Daring* so far from home and to hear of her heroic role,' he comments. 'When you help to build a ship it's part of you and you're part of it.' Johnny agrees with this sentiment. 'When a ship goes away a bit of you goes away,' he says.

Eddie adds: 'And a bit of that ship stays with you.'

A night time picture of the passenger liner **Vistafjord** *alongside the Neptune Yard shortly before her completion in 1973. She was built for the Norwegian America Line, but later sold to Cunard. Today she is* **Caronia***.*

Life in the Yards

The camaraderie and friendship at Swan's yards helped workers to overcome the difficulties they encountered as they built the ships. The warm humour and banter between them eased the pressures and the often arduous nature of the tasks.

Men worked on the open slipways in all weathers and in earlier years without hard helmets. Cold and wet conditions in winter and the need to be constantly vigilant because of the danger of accidents were among the negative aspects of the job.

Bob Koch, of South Shields, worked at the Wallsend Yard in the 1930s as a welder. He joined the yard in 1931 at the age of 18 and was trained in the job by Swan's. When he qualified, after three years, he was paid £3 a week.

Bob helped to carry out some of the pioneering electric welding work on Great Lake ships, including the *Joseph Medill*, a vessel which disappeared on her delivery voyage and is believed to have sunk during a storm off the north coast of Scotland. She, like the *Peter G. Campbell*, was one of the first vessels with an all-welded hull built on the Tyne.

Bob describes his six years at Swan's as 'marvellous' and remembers travelling to work across the Tyne on the Hebburn-Wallsend ferry. The ferry landing was situated next to the Wallsend Yard, close to the dry docks. This river crossing was used by many shipyard workers.

In the 1930s there were no safety helmets or safety guards on the sides of ships, nor were there any handrails for men to grip on to. The welders had to kneel down without pads. Later in life Bob was to have two knee operations. 'Sometimes you would use a bag with wood shavings in to kneel on.'

The training given by Swan's stood Bob in good stead. He remained a welder for the rest of his working life, serving also at Readhead's yard in South Shields and at Doxford's in Sunderland.

Norman Atkinson, of Brunswick Green, worked at Swan's during the Second World War, starting as an apprentice joiner

Norman Atkinson

Norman Atkinson, of Brunswick Green, who worked at Swan's during the Second World War, starting as an apprentice joiner aged 16 in 1939. Wartime needs sometimes required him to work a day and a night shift with only a couple of hours' break in between.

*HMS **Express**, a Swan's-built destroyer which was given a new bow at the Wallsend Dry Docks during the Second World War. Norman Atkinson recalls her arriving in the Tyne. Here, she is seen on her acceptance trials in 1934.*

to deal with them.

When the Swan's-built destroyer HMS *Express* came into the Tyne after having her bows blown off, a new bow was built at the Wallsend Yard. Norman saw the *Titan II* floating crane lift this new bow into one of the dry docks to be fitted to the ship.

Norman also recalls that ships were often moved down river from the yards to Wallsend Slipway and Engineering to have their engines and boilers installed.

Day shift hours during the Second World War were from 7.30am to 5.15pm. 'In the mornings, a second buzzer sounded at 7.35. If you missed getting to work by this time the gate was closed against you and you lost money.'

If an urgent job was needed during the war men might on occasions be called upon to do an ordinary day shift, then go home for their tea, and return at 7pm to work all night until 7am. Norman sometimes worked such hours. 'It was tiring, but the shifts were nothing compared with the ordeals servicemen and women were experiencing at the time,' he adds.

Bill Todd, of East Howdon, has shipbuilding in his blood. He was brought up in Gainers Terrace in the shadow of the Wallsend Shipyard and was born into a family whose livelihood depended on the industry. As a boy, he could see ships taking shape just a few yards from his bedroom window.

Shipbuilding had always been a central feature of Wallsend life. People living in nearby houses knew the yard was busy when they found it difficult to get to sleep because of the noise of riveters and caulkers.

in 1939 at the age of 16. He remembers helping to fit out destroyers, cruisers and the battleship HMS *Anson* at Wallsend. One of his jobs was to install the timber fittings for the radar offices aboard convoy escort vessels such as destroyers and frigates.

Norman and his workmates were drenched when an unexploded bomb went off close to the *Anson* as she lay alongside the jetty. The bomb had been dropped into the Tyne by a German aircraft during a raid the night before.

He recalls a few other bombing raids but says that often when the sirens went off it was a false alarm. The *Anson* was used as an air raid shelter by the workmen while she lay on the slipway. Her thick armour made her particularly suitable for this purpose.

The battleship was moved from Wallsend to the Walker Naval Yard to have her turrets fitted as these were immensely heavy and Swan's did not have a crane with the lifting capacity

Bill's father worked for Swan's as a welder and all his uncles were riveters. His cousin, Nancy Herdman, was one of the women employed at the Wallsend dry docks during the Second World War as a tack welder.

Against this background, it is hardly surprising that Bill also served in the yards, initially doing a spell as a welder and then training as a fitter with North East Marine.

He started at Swan's dry docks as a fitter in 1960 after leaving the RAF. Later he worked at the Wallsend Yard, again as a fitter, and served for a time in the drawing office.

Bill, who was a shop steward for the AEU at the dry docks and the shipyard, remembers that when he first began work with the company his wages were £12 10s a week, with overtime, for day shifts, which started at 7.30am. Clocking off time was 5pm. More money could be made on night shift, which lasted from 9pm to 7am.

Men at work on the bulbous bow of the supertanker **Esso Northumbria** *at the Wallsend yard in April 1969.*

He worked on Swan's supertankers, including *Esso Northumbria*. A fitter's job includes work on many aspects of vessels, such as valves, pipes, engines, boilers and winches. It was dangerous work. He escaped with minor injuries when he fell into a chain locker at the dry docks. Luckily the chain was still inside the locker as the ship had just docked and this broke his fall.

Bill says the job was often arduous and sometimes required great strength. Huge nuts aboard vessels in dry dock had to be

Frank Gray

Frank Gray, of Wallsend, who was a fitter until he was made redundant from Swan's in 1993.

loosened using large hammers which were struck against spanners. The job was 'freezing' in winter, with metal parts becoming extremely cold.

Frank Gray, a fitter, of Wallsend, also remembers those cold conditions. He served his apprenticeship in the Walker Naval Yard from 1965 to 1969. Frank then transferred to the Wallsend Yard, did a spell at Hawthorn Leslie's at Hebburn, and afterwards went to the Neptune Yard. He too tells of the large hammers used to tighten or loosen giant nuts connected to a 'flogging' spanner. 'It was heavy work.'

Frank worked on some of the supertankers and remembers the constant feeling of danger. Tanks aboard these huge ships were about 80ft or 90ft deep and safety nets were strung across them in case anyone fell in. He fitted large pipelines into tanks and on decks. Pipes could be as much as 28 inches in diameter.

Sometimes workers would be chosen to go with a ship on her trials. Frank was stationed in the engine room aboard the Swan's supertanker *Tyne Pride* when she went on trials en route to Hamburg for delivery. Such a trip was regarded as a bonus. It was a pleasure to sail in a vessel you had helped to build.

The working day at Neptune and Wallsend was punctuated by the familiar noise of the buzzers. These were sounded at the beginning and end of each shift. At home time the men would pour out of the gates in a flood. A sea of humanity would stream up the bank from the main entrance at Wallsend, a reminder that shipbuilding offered employment to many on Tyneside.

Edith Corby, of Monkseaton, was a teacher at Wallsend in the early 1950s. She remembers vividly the army of men who swarmed from the yard gates. 'The mass sound of their feet was tremendous. The first ones out would run up the bank towards the town.' The men were often dirty and greasy from their work. Edith's father, Alf Corby, worked at Swan's as a foreman shipwright during the Second World War and afterwards.

Edith told of how some men who lived near the Wallsend Yard went home for their lunch. 'I recall one man who lived in High Street West whose meal was always waiting on the table for him when he arrived home.'

The lunch break, from noon to 1pm, was also announced by the buzzers. Both the Wallsend and Neptune yards had canteens where, Frank says, 'you could get a reasonably priced, full meal'. Working on the slipways, he always had a good appetite when the break came.

Frank made many friends during his time with the company. 'When you came up against a difficult job the companionship helped to soothe things. The friendship was marvellous.' However, he never quite got used to the cold conditions working in winter. 'My feet were always freezing standing on the decks.'

Frank was made redundant from Swan's in 1993.

Les Hodgson, of Hadrian Park, Wallsend, joined the company as an apprentice plater in 1953 and, apart from his National Service, stayed in the yards until 1993 when he was made redundant. After serving his five-year apprenticeship, Les rose to become a head foreman.

He has memories of the 1950s when the yards were often shrouded in smoke from heavy industry and domestic fires. Dust filled the air in the workplace. Handrails and hard helmets had not been introduced.

Les recalls a man being killed after suffering a head injury while working on the *Bergensfjord* and another fatal

The workers look on as the 100,000 deadweight tons BP turbine tanker **British Argosy***, then the largest ship to be built in the North-East, enters the water at Wallsend on February 7 1960. Nearly 1,300 tons of drag chains were used to control the ship.*

Bobby Sisterson, of Longbenton, back row, centre, with workmates at the Walker Naval Yard c.1981. He worked as a coppersmith's labourer, plater's assistant and fireman during his time at the yards.

accident in which a man died when he fell from the top to the bottom of one of the tanks on a supertanker after someone had left a safety net open.

Another hazard, not fully appreciated at the time, was asbestos. This was often used in ship's bulkheads (walls). Les was sometimes called upon to work with this substance and one of his best friends died from an asbestos-related illness. 'I am told that research in America had revealed the dangers of asbestos before the Second World War,' he says.

The work could also involve being in confined spaces, such as the ship's double bottom. When he joined Swan's candles were still often used when carrying out tasks in such areas. 'If

you had a portable lamp that was a luxury.'

Les was head foreman in the fabrication shop for the *Illustrious* and *Ark Royal*. He also worked on five of the super-tankers. 'They were so huge it was time consuming to just get from one part of the ship to another. There was a lot of climbing, descending and walking.'

Bobby Sisterson, of Longbenton, began work at the Wallsend Yard in 1972 as a plater's helper, later becoming a fireman and coppersmith's labourer.

He says safety conditions gradually improved over the years. Eventually, hard helmets and safety boots were introduced as well as handrails on staging (scaffolding).

On one occasion, Bobby himself became a casualty. He was edging a bulkhead plate into position when the plate dropped on his hand, breaking two of his fingers and injuring his knuckles. He was off work for several weeks. In addition to Wallsend, Bobby also worked for four years at Neptune and took part in the fitting out of the *Ark Royal* and *Illustrious* at the Walker Naval Yard. The two huge ships were moved up river to Walker from Wallsend. He was employed as a coppersmith's labourer at the time, helping the craftsmen make piping.

Friendship was a feature of the offices as well as the slipways and fitting out quays. Carol Lawcock, of Whitley Bay, worked as secretary to Norman Parker, company secretary and commercial director, in the 1970s. She remembers Swan's as a 'family' type of firm where people looked after each other. 'I enjoyed it.'

Swan's at Play

Swan's staff were provided with a recreation and sports ground at Walkerville, close to Wallsend, which many of today's workforces would be happy to enjoy. It flourished before and after the Second World War and featured 18 acres of land, complete with football and rugby pitches, a cricket pitch, tennis courts and bowling greens.

Between the world wars hockey was also played there. In the late 1920s and the 1930s Swan's had a highly successful ladies hockey club and some of its members went on to play for the Northumberland ladies' teams. The company's 'A' team of the 1927-28 season, for example, played and won nine matches in succession, scoring a total of 88 goals. Their various opponents managed to notch up only six. This team was competing in the Newcastle Business Houses Ladies Hockey League.

A two-tier pavilion with a balcony was the centre of this sporting life. It was equipped with changing rooms, communal baths, and an upstairs social hall.

A second pavilion, used mainly by the successful rugby club, was opened in the 1960s. Sometimes bowls players and cricketers would also use this building. Drawing office man Eddie Jackson recalls that the extensive grounds featured flower beds and a pond, which had once been a paddling pool. 'Our pitches were never too water-logged after rain or snow because the pond acted as a drain. But it was eventually filled in.'

Les Hodgson played rugby for Swan's club from the 1950s to the 1970s. During the Second World War his father had been captain of one of the teams. He remembers the pitches as being among the best on Tyneside. The first team pitch was 'like playing on a carpet'.

A full-time groundsman was employed who lived in a house on the site. The greens and pitches were thus well maintained. The site also featured a bandstand which was used by the Wallsend Shipyard Band in the period between the two world wars. This enabled the musicians to get in plenty of practice for launches. In the 1920s and 1930s the band sometimes played at Newcastle United's St James's Park on match days and also entered competitions and gave concerts at other venues.

Eddie tells of the Swan Hunter motoring club which existed in the 1960s. 'So-called treasure hunts were organised. These

Good players. Swan's Ladies Hockey 'A' team of the 1927-28 season.

Cup winners. The highly successful Swan's apprentices football team of the 1929-30 season.

Wallsend Yard. The institute was also a venue for billiards competitions. In addition to all these activities, apprentices between the wars had the chance to go on an annual summer camp at Newbiggin-by-the-Sea, Northumberland.

The year 1930 provides an interesting insight into the nature of this sporting and social life.

The annual staff dance was held at the Wallsend Memorial Hall on January 31, *The Shipyard* magazine describing it as a 'delightful' evening. It declared: 'After supper, dancing was resumed with renewed enthusiasm, and the spotlight came into play, lending just that last touch of romance which the young couples so much enjoy. Prizes for spot dancing were awarded to Mr Logie and Miss Turnbull, Mr Lough and Miss Farthing.' After all expenses had been met for the event, the sum of £8 12s 6d was handed over to the Royal Victoria Infirmary, Newcastle.

On May 30 the ladies of the Wallsend Office played a spirited bowls match against their men colleagues on the greens at the recreation ground. *The Shipyard* commented wryly: 'Once on the green, it was obvious to the male sex that it would require something more than a few quiet draws to win the match. In fact, it must be truthfully stated here and now that the game as played by either side was by no means free from bias.' However, the men did, with some difficulty, manage to pull off a victory, with the ladies holding them to a draw on one rink.

The Swan's apprentices' football team, which played in the Tyneside Works Welfare League, finished the 1929-30 season as runners-up for top honours in the league and won the cup competition. They were victorious in 14 games out of 20 played, with three matches being drawn. The team scored a total of 71 goals.

On May 27 the recreation ground saw the annual cricket match between the clerks and draughtsmen of the Wallsend Yard. The clerks managed to regain possession of the cup which had eluded them for two years. On June 2 the Wallsend East Yard foremen competed in a bowls match against their counterparts from the Wallsend West Yard. The men of the West Yard won by 99 to 71 points.

were leisurely car rallies in the countryside in which members would hunt for wooden rabbits. It was great fun.'

Staff of the company also attended dances, many of which were held at the Wallsend Memorial Hall. The building of the hall was paid for by the directors and employees of the company as a tribute to the Swan's workers who lost their lives in the First World War. It was opened in 1925. A fine memorial by North-East sculptor Roger Hedley, son of Victorian Newcastle artist Ralph Hedley, is still a feature of the building's exterior in Frank Street. Beautiful statues of a soldier and sailor flank the inscriptions.

Between the wars whist drives, occasionally combined with dances, were popular, some being held at the recreation ground pavilion and others at the Staff Institute building at the

Three days later, a Saturday, Wallsend foremen went on their annual outing, together with their wives and families. A party of 90, assembling at the Memorial Hall, were taken on a trip to Bamburgh by coaches. On their way home they stopped off at Seahouses and a collection was held, the money being handed over to the local lifeboat fund.

This donation was by no means an isolated event. Swan's workers were generous in giving to medical charities. Committees of workmen were set up mainly for this purpose at both Wallsend and Neptune, with considerable sums of money being collected for hospitals and other medical institutions.

For example, in most years between the wars they donated hundreds of pounds to the Royal Victoria Infirmary in Newcastle. Money was also given to the Walker Accident Hospital and the Fleming Memorial Hospital for Sick Children as well as numerous other North-East hospitals.

Charity could, of course, take forms additional to raising money. On July 19 1930 members of the Wallsend Yard Workmen's Committee, with their wives and friends, paid their annual visit to the children's sanatorium at Stannington, Northumberland. The shipyard band played and each boy and girl was presented with a box of sweets. In addition, toys were presented to the youngsters who were bed patients.

Les Hodgson

Rugby team. Les Hodgson, second row, centre, and other rugby team members in 1979. Norman Gilchrist, who became production director, is second row, far right.

From Boom to Uncertainty

The years immediately following the Second World War were prosperous ones for Swan's as companies sought to replace ships lost in the conflict.

Notable vessels constructed during this period included the passenger liners *Gothic*, completed in 1948 for Shaw, Savill and Albion Line, the *Provence*, launched at Neptune in 1950 for the French SGTM Line, and the Norwegian America Line's *Bergensfjord*, launched in 1955 at Wallsend. She featured an extensive aluminium superstructure and beautiful interior decoration by Scandinavian artists.

Besides such prestigious ships, the yards also turned out more mundane vessels, such as the Norwegian oil tanker *Vestfold*, the Blue Funnel cargo liner *Jason*, and the Cunard cargo liner *Assyria*, all completed in early 1950.

In 1960 the Neptune Yard saw the launch of the Portuguese passenger liner *Principe Perfeito*. She was built for service between Portugal and Mozambique.

Between 1955 and 1965 17 cargo ships, all of similar design, were built for the Europe-West Africa service, 12 of these being for the Palm Line. In addition, the early 1960s saw five cargo ships constructed for the Clan Line. These were all medium-sized vessels.

However, ocean going giants were soon to make their appearance on the slipways. Between 1968 and 1976 Swan's built eight supertankers at Wallsend. At around 250,000 dead-weight tonnes, they were the largest ships ever launched on the Tyne. The first of these giants, *Esso Northumbria*, towered over terraced houses in Wallsend's Leslie Street which was situated next to the yard. *Esso Northumbria* was launched by Princess Anne in 1969.

As the ship entered the river she was slowed down and prevented from hitting the opposite bank by a combination of tugs and 1,750 tons of drag chains. To create more leeway for the giant vessel, a section of the Hebburn bank was removed. Even so, the stern of the vessel came within 20ft of the bank.

Thousands turned out to watch the launch and also to watch *Esso Northumbria* depart from the Tyne on her delivery voyage in February 1970. The other supertankers included *Esso Hibernia*, *Texaco Great Britain*, *World Unicorn* and *Tyne Pride*. These huge ships, particularly *Esso Northumbria*, are well remembered on Tyneside.

Vessels were also produced for the Royal Fleet Auxiliary Service. In 1965 the company completed the 'O' class RFA tanker *Olmeda* and between 1969 and 1974 five RFA Rover Class small fleet tankers.

In 1966 Swan's amalgamated with John Readhead & Sons of South Shields and then with the Walker Naval Yard of Vickers and Hawthorn Leslie of Hebburn, all renowned Tyne shipbuilders. Smith's Dock Ltd., a leading shiprepairer on the Tyne and which had a shipbuilding yard on Teesside, also became part of the Swan's group.

In 1969 Swan's took over the Haverton Hill yard on the Tees. In addition, Palmer's Dry Dock (also known as Hebburn Dry Dock) was bought by Swan's from Vickers in 1973. In 1977, the company, by this time named Swan Hunter Shipbuilders Ltd., was nationalised, remaining under public ownership until privatisation in 1986.

Meanwhile, other notable vessels had been launched. The year 1973 saw the completion of the Norwegian passenger ship *Vistafjord* at Neptune.

*A crowd at the launch of **Esso Hibernia** at the Wallsend Shipyard in 1969. She was the second of eight supertankers built at the yard between 1968 and 1976. More than 30,000 tons of steel were used in her construction.*

*The aircraft carrier HMS **Illustrious** five days after her Wallsend Yard launch in December 1978. The **Titan II** floating crane is alongside.*

In 1978 Swan's completed HMS *Newcastle*, the first of a new breed of guided missile destroyers, the Type-42s, to be built at Neptune. She was followed by her sister ships, HMS *Glasgow* and HMS *Exeter*. Tragically, eight men working on the *Glasgow* died when fire broke out aboard in 1976.

In 1988 the landing ship RFA *Sir Galahad* was delivered from Wallsend. She was ordered to replace her namesake which was attacked during the Falklands War with tragic consequences at Bluff Cove in 1982. The replacement is a larger vessel capable of carrying more than 300 soldiers and their vehicles.

By the 1980s Swan's was forced to rely increasingly on warship orders. Even so, there were a few merchant vessels built. The Neptune Yard, which had turned out many of the world's cableships, completed its final cableship, the *Pacific Guardian*, in 1984 for Cable & Wireless. She was the 24th vessel of this type to slide down the yard's ways.

Swan's greatest achievement in warship building came with the construction of two of the Royal Navy's three modern aircraft carriers, HMS *Ark Royal* and HMS *Illustrious*. They remain among the company's most prestigious ships.

Illustrious was launched into the Tyne at the Wallsend Yard by Princess Margaret in December 1978. The vessel was then moved up river to the Walker Naval Yard for fitting out.

As relations with Argentina deteriorated in the spring of 1982, the Royal Navy requested that her completion be speeded up. The workforce rose to the challenge and pulled out all the stops. They upheld Swan's reputation as one of the world's greatest shipbuilders by completing this highly complex modern aircraft carrier 12 weeks ahead of schedule. *Illustrious* sailed from the Tyne in June, 1982, with crowds lining the banks of the river to bid her farewell. She joined the second wave of ships assigned to the Falklands task force.

The *Ark Royal* was launched at the Wallsend Yard in June 1981 by the Queen Mother. Like her sister, she was also fitted out at the Walker Naval Yard. The ship was ready for sea trials by October 1984 and was delivered the following year.

During the 1980s and early 1990s the company's workforce

The RFA **Fort George** on the slipway at Wallsend shortly before her launch in 1991.

Stan Gamester

Wallsend Yard drawing office staff with a computer image of the Antarctic research ship **James Clark Ross.** *The ship was a technical triumph for Swan Hunter but was built at a loss and contributed to the company's problems.*

was engaged on the building of a series of anti-submarine frigates for the Royal Navy, the Type-22s HMS *Sheffield*, HMS *Coventry* and HMS *Chatham* and the Type-23s HMS *Westminster*, HMS *Northumberland* and HMS *Richmond*. In January 1988 the *Chatham* became the last ship to be launched from the Neptune Yard and afterwards construction and launching of hulls was switched entirely to Wallsend.

Swan's had been privatised in 1986 in a £5 million buy-out by management. The company was officially designated a warship builder as part of the deal which meant that it was disqualified from obtaining European Commission subsidies for merchant shipbuilding. This lack of funding seriously disadvantaged it when competing for merchant vessel orders with shipyards worldwide which did receive subsidies.

Other problems also arose. Not long after privatisation, the company failed to win an order for the fleet oil ship RFA *Fort Victoria*. Instead, the contract went to Harland and Wolff at Belfast. Swan's directors believed the competition had not been fair since the Belfast yard had received £37 million in subsidies and had not built a warship for many years. Evidence was to emerge that the government's desire to promote peace in Northern Ireland had influenced its decision. However, Swan's did manage to win the contract for her sister ship, *Fort George*, launched at Wallsend in 1991. Four more RFA ships planned by the MoD were abandoned because of defence spending cuts.

Meanwhile, the company had won two merchant ship orders despite the lack of subsidies. The Wallsend Yard launched its one and only cableship, the *Sir Eric Sharp*, in 1988, for Cable & Wireless. Swan's 24 other cableships were from the Neptune slipways. Then came a merchant vessel which brought with it the first hint of financial disaster. In December 1990 the Queen launched an Antarctic research ship, the *James Clark Ross*, at Wallsend. This state-of-the-art vessel was a wonderful example of how the workforce could turn out a technically excellent, specialised vessel, yet she was built at a loss and weakened Swan's financial position.

It was also beset by another problem. Following completion of the RFA *Fort George* the company was involved in a dispute with the Ministry of Defence over full payment of £20 million it claimed was owed for extra work done on the ship. This situation increased the fragility of the shipbuilder's finances.

A cloud was gathering over the Wallsend Yard. The end of the Cold War which had led to reduced defence spending had sparked fierce competition between Britain's yards for increasingly scarce orders. In addition, there were no merchant ship subsidies for Wallsend. A situation arose in which the fate of the old Swan's company, now in millions of pounds debt, would hang upon the thread of securing one order.

The Time of Trouble

In 1993 came the blow which plunged Swan's into receivership. It failed to win the order for the helicopter carrier HMS *Ocean* and mass redundancies followed.

HMS *Ocean* was a vessel Swan's could have built to the highest standards and it was an order it should have won. The company could draw on one of the most experienced design teams in the world and the men on the slipways were of a high calibre, skilled, experienced, well motivated and imbued with a strong sense of Geordie pride.

Their forefathers possessed that same pride, which had forged the Tyne's reputation for fine shipbuilding. Indeed, over generations, sons had followed fathers into the yards. The skills and energy of the river had given Britain unsurpassed service in both war and peace. But the pride and the effort, as well as the skill, were to be of no avail.

The stance taken by an unhelpful Conservative government contributed greatly to Swan's downfall. The superb work done on warships by Swan's men, which was praised by the Royal Navy, seemed to count for little with ministers who had the power to give the company the helicopter carrier order and thus save people's jobs.

VSEL of Barrow, Cumbria, in a consortium with Kvaerner-Govan on the Clyde, undercut Swan's bid by £71 million and was awarded the contract for HMS *Ocean*. Swan's had bid £210 million and VSEL-Kvaerner-Govan £139 million. But was the winning bid realistic? At Swan's many people felt that their rival's tender was unrealistically low. The key question was: Why was VSEL able to bid £71 million less than Swan's?

The work of building the helicopter carrier's hull was carried out by Kvaerner-Govan, a company with no experience of

Stan Gamester

Uncertain future. A worker begins his walk up Swan's Bank after being made redundant in 1993.

constructing such a warship, unlike Swan's which had launched the *Ark Royal* and *Illustrious*. VSEL installed HMS *Ocean*'s armaments systems.

However, although VSEL and Kvaerner-Govan had bid £139 million, the bill for the work was to soar to over £200m. A spares and maintenance contract, not mentioned publicly at the time of the bids, plus inflation were said by the government to have contributed to the huge increase. The government maintained that such extra costs would have been added on to Swan's original bid.

In 1996 a National Audit Office report said the final figure would be £201 million. This did not take into account the cost of damage to HMS *Ocean*'s hull, received during her launch on the Clyde. The *Ocean* was completed in 1998.

Dick Gonsalez, who was chairman of Wallsend Yard branch of the Confederation of Shipbuilding and Engineering Unions, says: 'No one seems to be able to come up with the exact figure for the final cost. Politicians who said they wanted value for money suddenly seemed unconcerned about the cost. I still feel bitter. Over 2,000 people on Tyneside were robbed of their livelihoods.'

Dick is firmly against the attitude which consigns British heavy industry to history. This, he believes, is a negative approach which has been adopted by many politicians. He says shipbuilding, engineering and similar heavy industrial trades provided the skills base for the country's prosperity.

On May 13 1993 Swan's management called in the receivers following the loss of the order. Around 2,400 jobs were now in jeopardy. Soon afterwards 450 workers were made redundant. The shock reverberated around the North-East. The receivers said they would try to sell the company as a going concern.

Generations of men had walked up Swan's Bank on their way home from the Wallsend Yard. Now, those made redundant walked that same route, but with their livelihoods gone and an uncertain future.

In July the Ministry of Defence agreed that Swan's could complete the three frigates then under construction, *Westminster*, *Northumberland* and *Richmond*. Also in July, a further 286 people lost their jobs. In September, the company failed to win an Omani gunboat order. Instead, it went to French company CMN. The same month saw 80 more workers made redundant, followed by 510 in November when the *Westminster* was completed.

Stan Gamester

A vigorous campaigner. Dick Gonsalez, who was chairman of Wallsend Yard branch of the Confederation of Shipbuilding and Engineering Unions. He helped to lead the campaign to save Swan's.

In December, the European Commission granted Swan's merchant shipbuilding subsidies. But it was too late.

By early 1994 French shipbuilder CMN had expressed an interest in buying the company. In March of that year the receivers put in a bid to refit the landing ship *Sir Bedivere*. CMN said the award of the contract would be a condition of any takeover. But the government gave the order to Rosyth Dockyard. It had pledged itself to place 50 per cent of all surface ship refits with the Scottish yard.

In May, 148 more workers were made redundant and there were 235 lay-offs, coinciding with the completion of HMS *Northumberland*.

CMN, however, did not drop their interest in acquiring Swan's. They submitted a new takeover proposal, but this collapsed when the Ministry of Defence cut £350,000 off the amount it had originally agreed to pay CMN for completion of HMS *Richmond*.

The move was another blow dealt by the government to a company which had given such sterling service to Britain. The decision had been taken to save a mere £350,000, a trifling sum in warship building terms. Surely, people asked, this sum was a price worth paying to save the yard and the jobs of over 2,000 workers?

Richmond, the final ship built by the old Swan's company, was launched in April 1993. The traditional three cheers were given for the vessel as she slid down the ways at the Wallsend Yard where so many great ships had been launched before.

But behind the pride there were tears. Men had worked under immense pressure to the best of their ability to produce the last batch of ships in the knowledge they had no guarantee of a job after the contracts were finished. These vessels sailed from the river as fine examples of Wallsend's expertise. In the circumstances, the achievement of the Swan's workforce was

Stan Gamester

Two of the last apprentices with the old Swan's company at a Save Our Swan's campaign mass meeting at the Wallsend Yard in late 1993.

even more remarkable.

A small Shields ferry boat, aptly named *Pride of the Tyne*, was the last of the old Swan Hunter company's vessels to enter the river but she cannot be described as a ship. Built at Wallsend, she was lifted into the water by a crane in June 1993. It was a strange irony that the very first vessel in the company's long history had also been a small ferry, the paddle steamer *Victoria*.

A Phoenix from the Ashes

When the *Richmond* departed from Wallsend on November 3 1994 there were tears among the workers and their families who witnessed the event. A feeling of injustice swept them. There was a sense of loss, a mourning for a way of life that seemed at the time to have ended. Shipbuilding has indeed been part of the Geordie consciousness, a proud element of the industry and culture of Tyneside upon which the livelihoods of many families have depended.

As the *Richmond* moved away from her fitting-out quay the shipyard band played for the last time, the strains of *Now is the Hour* and *Auld Lang Syne* drifting out over the Tyne amid rain as if sounding a lament for the river's troubled shipbuilding industry.

Sailors aboard the departing frigate stood on deck and, waving their caps, gave three cheers to the men who had put

Stan Gamester

*Yard men on the bow of HMS **Richmond** as she nears completion at Wallsend in 1994. She was the last ship completed by the old Swan Hunter company. Today a new company, Swan Hunter (Tyneside) Ltd., has risen from the ashes of the old.*

all their energy and skill into creating their ship. It was a moving tribute. The Ministry of Defence's principal naval overseer for *Richmond* and her captain praised the standard of the workmanship.

The departure signalled more redundancies and now only 125 workers were left at the yard. By this time, the Hebburn Dry Dock and the Neptune Yard had been acquired by other companies for shiprepair. Only Wallsend remained as the last outpost of the once great Swan's empire. Now its berths were strangely empty, its giant cranes stilled by decisions taken beyond the Tyne. The yard resembled a concrete and metal desert, silent and bereft of life. A precious national asset had been brought to the verge of extinction.

During the crisis the Confederation of Shipbuilding and Engineering Unions had launched a vigorous campaign to save Swan's, backed by the North-East community, MPs, local councils and Tyneside newspapers. Now, with the last vessel gone, the campaigners pledged to continue the fight to bring shipbuilding back to Wallsend.

Dick Gonsalez, who together with councillor Eddie Darke played a leading role in the campaign, says: 'The way the people of the North-East community, north and south of the river, rallied round to support the campaign was tremendous.'

Eventually almost all the 2,400 workers employed by the company lost their jobs, with only a small skeleton staff being retained by receivers Price Waterhouse. The knock-on effects of the redundancies were also believed to be significant. It was estimated at the time that up to 6,000 more people might lose their livelihoods because supply and service businesses would be hit.

Swan's workers felt they had been the victims of an uncaring and indifferent government. All they had

An aerial view of the river frontage at Wallsend and Walker from the cover of **The Shipyard Magazine** *for July - August, 1933.*

The first number of **The Shipyard Magazine** *was issued in February 1919, priced one penny. Its aim was to: 'consider in a broadminded way social, economic and religious questions, to foster the spirit of comradeship and good understanding between employers and employed and so develop that unity which is so necessary to progress and well being, especially in these momentous days'.*

Solitaire, which was converted into the world's largest pipe-laying vessel at Swan Hunter's Wallsend Shipyard.

wanted was to retain their jobs. Many were forced to find lower paid work away from Tyneside, often on a casual or short-term contract basis, and travel home at weekends. Their wages were eroded by this travel and by accommodation costs. Family life was severely disrupted.

Temporary, lower-paid work, often without paid holidays, was no substitute for a regular job and higher wage at a shipyard such as Swan's. But by this time the industry was changing. Temporary employment was becoming the norm.

A number of staff from the design department eventually found work with VSEL in Cumbria. Some workers were forced to go abroad in their quest for a job. Others had great difficulty in securing any employment at all and if they did it might be unconnected with their skills.

The talented and highly experienced workforce of the world renowned Wallsend Yard was thus dispersed.

In 1995 a survey carried out by Dr John Tomaney, of Newcastle University, which was commissioned by Radio 5 Live, found that the majority of former Swan's workers were still unemployed. Over half had been jobless since being made redundant. More than two thirds of those in employment had temporary contracts.

Some had had up to five jobs in 18 months.

The Conservative government did not believe in apportioning the work to Britain's yards so that jobs could be saved. Instead, it backed the concept of giving the work to the lowest bidder despite the cost in terms of unemployment.

The idea of granting Swan's a contract because it was a company with great expertise and a proven track record, employed many people and was a national asset which should be preserved for future shipbuilding needs, seemed unimportant to ministers against their desire to save money. It was, of course, taxpayers' money, but Swan's workers were taxpayers too.

In May 1995 Defence Minister Roger Freeman was reported to have told the Commons Defence Select Committee the government had decided it was not appropriate to allocate orders to the company.

Swan's workforce had put all their pride and effort into building ships for the Royal Navy. They had completed a sophisticated vessel such as the carrier *Illustrious* well ahead of schedule to help Britain during the Falklands crisis. Yet, it was pointed out, when Swan's was fighting for survival ministers had refused to give Swan's work. It was a formidable blow to people's livelihoods and to their way of life. But their proud record of turning out soundly built ships of high quality over 130 years could not be taken away from them.

Many along the banks of the river believed the Conservative government had abandoned the company because Labour support on Tyneside was overwhelming. The situation was not likely to be changed by saving the river's last remaining shipbuilder. There was only one Conservative seat, Tynemouth, and that was won by Labour in the 1997 general election, a major factor in this Conservative defeat being their treatment of Swan's.

But the Wallsend Yard was not finished, nor was shipbuilding on the Tyne. A new Swan's was to arise from the ashes of the old. The receivers continued with their quest to find a buyer and were eventually successful. The Dutch-owned THC group purchased the yard for £5 million in June 1995. This eleventh-hour deal was struck only days before an auction of the yard's equipment was due to begin. Swan's had been in receivership for over two years.

A new company was formed to operate the yard, Swan Hunter (Tyneside) Ltd., headed by Dutch businessman Jaap Kroese.

Soon the Wallsend Yard was stirring again. Within months, it had won an order to convert the merchant ship *Solitaire* into the world's largest pipe-laying vessel. This gave work to 3,000 men for a period of 20 months. Then, in late 2000, the company secured a deal to convert a tanker, *Global Producer*, into a floating oil production and storage vessel (FPSO) for the North Sea. This gave 800 men jobs for at least 12 months.

Shortly afterwards, came the first order to build, rather than convert, ships at the Wallsend yard since the collapse of the old Swan's. The new Swan Hunter was awarded a Ministry of Defence contract for the construction of two 16,000-tonne amphibious landing vessels, the *Largs Bay* and *Lyme Bay*. It was expected the landing ships deal would provide, at the height of the work, around 2,000 jobs. Meanwhile, Cammell Laird's yard, at Hebburn, built a roll-on roll-off ferry for Norwegian owners.

The two Royal Fleet Auxiliary landing vessels *Largs Bay* and *Lyme Bay* were each built by the new Swan's within a floating dock placed within a specially excavated 'inland harbour', similar to a dry dock but always containing water. The vessels were launched by moving the floating dock out of the inland harbour and then sinking the dock into the Tyne until the ships became water-borne. *Largs Bay* was the first to be launched in this unusual way and was delivered in April 2006.

However, delays and escalating costs on the project led the Ministry of Defence to order that her sister ship, *Lyme Bay*, be towed from the Tyne to the Clyde for completion. She departed the yard in July 2006. It was claimed in some media reports that *Lyme Bay* was the only ship ever to leave the river uncompleted but this was inaccurate.

Swan's had suffered from the design teething problems associated with being the lead yard for this class of vessel. Things did not go well. Difficulties arose with adapting a Dutch shipyard design to the requirements of the British Ministry of Defence. The situation was not helped by one of the ship's engines suffering water damage during work at the yard. Costs soared.

However, Mr Kroese had saved shipbuilding on the Tyne from virtual extinction for over a decade, providing much needed jobs and reviving the training of apprentices. Without Mr Kroese's intervention the Wallsend Yard would have closed in 1995. He had been the only entrepreneur plucky enough to save it and he gave the yard an extra 11 years of working life.

By summer 2008, most of the great cranes of Swan Hunter at Wallsend had disappeared from the Tyneside skyline. They had been sold to the Bharati Shipbuilding company in India. The sale included the *Titan III* floating crane. The loss of the cranes was mourned by many people. A sad gap was left in the skyline of Tyneside, but the name Swan Hunter will forever have a premier place in the history of shipbuilding.

Partly dismantled cranes at the Wallsend Yard, early 2008.

Ships and their Stories

BATHORY

In the autumn of 1891 the Neptune yard received a large order for 14 ships to be built for the Royal Hungarian Adria Steam Navigation of Fiume. Five more ships were ordered some months later. These small cargo ships were built to trade from Austro-Hungarian ports to Marseilles, Spain and Brazil. The photograph shows the *Bathory*, which was completed in 1892. She is seen driven aground north of Port Patrick in south west Scotland on December 3 1897, when en-route to Glasgow. The ship was battered by westerly gales and heavy seas for three months. She was eventually salvaged and towed to Glasgow, where she was repaired and returned to service. *Bathory* was sunk by the British cruiser HMS *Minerva* on September 1 1914 off the coast of Vigo, Spain.

NEUNFELS

For almost 100 years Deutsche DG *Hansa* was one of Germany's most famous cargo liner companies. Up to the outbreak of the First World War the Neptune yard had built 28 ships for them, a quarter of their fleet. Their trade was to the Indian sub-continent and to the gulf ports of the USA. One of these ships, the *Neunfels*, pictured, was launched on April 19 1901. During the First World War the *Neunfels* was discharging her cargo in a Spanish port when she was detained. A prize court awarded her to Spain after the war as partial reparation for losses suffered by the Spanish. In 1921 when named *Espana No. 6* work began on converting her into a seaplane/balloon ship for the Spanish Navy and she was renamed the *Dedalo*. The ship was capable of operating 25 seaplanes and two 130-ft airships. In 1925 the *Dedalo* was used during the Spanish invasion of Morocco. In 1939 she was towed to Valencia but sank at the berth and was blown up to clear the harbour.

PROVENCE

The 15,700-ton French passenger liner *Provence*, pictured, completed in 1951, was the 10th ship built for her owners at the Neptune Yard. She was constructed for a passenger service to South America, sailing from her home port of Marseilles. In September 1954 she was in collision in the River Plate estuary with the Liberian tanker *Saxonsea*. Extensively damaged, the liner made it back to her home port for repairs. *Provence* resumed her service until 1961 when she was given a major refit, after which the service became a joint operation with the Italian Costa Lines. Her home port was changed to *Genoa*. Her French owners went into liquidation in 1965 and Costa bought the ship. After further modifications the ship was renamed *Enrico C* and resumed service on the South Atlantic run. Later, the ship's role was changed to cruising, alternating between South American

waters in the winter and Europe in the summer. In 1987 she was renamed *Enrico Costa* and in 1990 underwent a refit at Genoa after a major engine failure. Following the repairs the ship went back to cruising. In 1965 the *Enrico Costa* was sold to another Italian cruise company, the Star Lauro Line, who renamed her *Symphony* and put her on cruises to South Africa. At the turn of the millennium she was still in service.

CITY OF PARIS

The Wallsend Yard built 22 ships for the Ellerman Line. One of the more important was the *City of Paris*, pictured. This cargo-passenger liner was launched in December 1920. She had accommodation for 349 passengers for the UK-India service. Before she could be completed, however, there was a lengthy strike by joiners. The owners demanded delivery, she ran trials in an incomplete state off the Tyne in September 1921, and then proceeded to St Nazaire to be finished off by the Pehoet shipyard, finally being handed over in February 1922. Initially *City of Paris* made two round trips to Japan, before settling down to her designed route, which she maintained until 1936 when she was switched to the UK - South African service. Two years later she was sent for a major refit. In September 1939, when returning from Cape Town, she struck a magnetic mine in the Thames estuary, which caused considerable damage. She was the

first recorded victim of this type of weapon. For the duration of the war *City of Paris* was used as a troopship worldwide. After the war she was used for floating accommodation at Hong Kong for port workmen. In 1947 she returned to Wallsend and was greatly modernised, after which she re-entered the South African service, which she was kept on for the next eight years. By this time she was getting old and was replaced by the superb looking *City of Port Elizabeth* quartet of ships, completed at the Walker Naval Yard in 1953. The *City of Paris,* having served her country well, was broken up at Newport in 1956.

JOHN W. MACKAY

The *John W. Mackay*, pictured, was one of a pair of cableships built in 1925 for the Commercial Cable Co. of London. Up to the start of World War II she laid various transatlantic cables, and during the conflict was commissioned by the Admiralty and operated in the Persian Gulf and Pacific. During one operation later in the war she spent three weeks lifting 450 miles of Italian cable off the seabed close to the Cape Verde Islands. After the war the *John W. Mackay* spent most of her time laying and repairing North Atlantic links. From 1965 to 1976 she worked worldwide. In 1977 the ship was finally laid up at Greenwich on the Thames after 52 years of service. While moored there she was used several times as a static movie set. Various plans were made for her future, including a proposal to turn her into a museum ship for the telecommunications industry funded by a trust. In 1989 she returned to the Tyne for conversion work to be carried out by the training company Amarc in the dry dock on

the site of the former Hawthorn Leslie shipyard. The ship languished in the dock for five years as the trust scoured various sources for additional funding. But it was to no avail. Other schemes were mooted to preserve the old ship but these failed to materialise. It is sad that the *John W. Mackay*, a fine example of a Swan's cableship, which could have been a floating museum on the Tyne, had to be sent to the breaker's yard after a highly useful career.

HOPESTAR

It was common practice for shipbuilding companies and UK ship owners to hold shares in each other's businesses to protect their interests etc. The Swan Hunter organisation had a substantial stake in the Hopemount Shipping Co. Ltd. From 1903 the company built 21 cargo tramps for the company for worldwide operation and one oil tanker. One of this fleet was the *Hopestar*, pictured, launched on January 22 1936, without ceremony as a mark of respect for the recently dead King George V. After a visit to the dry docks for repairs *Hopestar* sailed from the Tyne on November 2 1948, bound for Philadelphia. For some time she had been fitted out with weather monitoring equipment, reporting back at regular intervals to the Air Ministry in London. On the 14th the ship radioed her agents, reporting structural damage sustained by heavy weather. Nothing more was heard of her again or her 40 crew, despite an extensive search by the U.S. Coastguards. At the Ministry of Transport inquiry into her loss it was found that the ship's structural integrity had been compromised, due to the cutting away of deck plating at the dockyard to install a new ship's boiler and other modifications.

ELINGAMITE

Elingamite which was built at Wallsend in the 1880s, was one of a series of ships launched for Australian owners for their coastwise and trans-Tasman Sea routes to New Zealand. *Elingamite* is an aboriginal name meaning 'water'. The ship sailed from the Tyne on September 24 1887 bound for London to load cargo for her outward passage. Initially the vessel, which could carry 280 passengers, was used on the Newcastle (New South Wales) to Melbourne route, but two years later switched to the Melbourne to New Zealand service. In 1893 her home port was switched to Sydney. During the closing years of the century she made several runs to Western Australia taking prospectors and goods out to the gold fields. On November 5 1902 she left Sydney bound for Auckland with 136 passengers, and 52 boxes of bullion belonging to a bank. Four days later when approaching the northern tip of New Zealand *Elingamite* encountered heavy fog. Disaster struck when the ship ran aground at West King Island. She sank within 20 minutes with the loss of 89 lives. At the court of inquiry the captain's certificate was suspended and he was fined £50. It was not until many years later that it was discovered the charts were wrong, and this exonerated the captain. The isolated position of the wreck and the heavy seas which pound the area made recovery of the bullion hazardous, leading to the death of several divers. Most of the gold remains on the seabed to this day.

HMS ALBION

The aircraft carrier HMS *Albion*, pictured, was laid down in March 1944. As the war evolved so did the Admiralty's requirements, and steel and equipment used for her construction were diverted to more pressing causes. The build programme was therefore put on the backburner and construction progressed slowly. In October 1949 *Albion* was being towed to Rosyth, where she spent several long periods in dry dock over the years. On her voyage north she broke adrift from the tugs in a gale close to the Longstone Lighthouse in the Farne Islands. As she ran free in the storm she collided with a small collier, the *Maystone,* and only four of the collier's crew were saved. The *Albion* was eventually handed over to the Royal Navy at Wallsend in March 1953. Her duties alternated between the Mediterranean and Far Eastern fleets, and she was on station during the Anglo-French operations in the Suez Crisis of 1956. In 1961 work started on converting her into a commando carrier for a rapid reaction force of 680 Marines. In the nine years she served in the role she had three commissions with the Far East Fleet. In 1970 *Albion* was paid off into the reserve

fleet. In 1973 she was reported as being sold to a Middlesbrough company, who planned to use her for the North Sea oil fields. The plan failed to materialise and the ship was towed to the breakers at Faslane later that year.

BRITISH STAR (renamed OLYNTHUS)

The BP Tanker Company was formed in 1915, by the Anglo-Iranian Oil Co., who had obtained a contract to ship vast amounts of oil back to the UK to fuel the Royal Navy and industry for the war effort. By the end of the First World War the company had either built or bought 22 ships, one of these being the *British Star*. Large for her day, she could carry 10,000 tons of cargo, and was delivered to her owners from Swan's in March 1918. Three days later she sailed from the Tyne in convoy . When 1.5 miles from the piers *British Star* was torpedoed by a U-boat, but was able to return to the river for repairs. The ship was bought by the Admiralty in 1922 to transport oil from the refineries to Admiralty storage depots worldwide. She was eventually renamed *Olynthus*. When the Second World War broke out *Olynthus* was upgraded to support oiler for the fleet, and attached to the South Atlantic cruiser squadron, refuelling the cruisers HMS *Ajax* and HMS *Achilles* as they searched for the German pocket battleship *Graf Spee*. It was during this time that she received the following message from the area Commander in Chief: 'If *Graf Spee* comes your way let her through.' It can be imagined what the crew's comments were when they heard the message. After the war *Olynthus* was sold to an Italian company who operated her until 1960 when she was broken up.

HMS LAMERTON

The Hunt class destroyers became the workhorses of the fleet during the Second World War, with 28 of these 1100-ton ships being launched on the Tyne and half of these were built at the Wallsend Yard. A typical example was HMS *Lamerton*, pictured, completed in August 1941. Her initial deployment was in the Western Approaches, protecting convoys in the UK sector of the North Atlantic, during which she sank an Italian submarine. In 1942 she was active in protecting the convoys to Russia, and hindering German shipping operations along the Norwegian coast. The ship was damaged in a collision when escorting a troop convoy in the Mediterranean in July 1942. After repairs she spent the next two years with the Mediterranean Fleet, supporting the landings in North Africa. In 1943 HMS *Lamerton* was used for gunfire support during the invasion of Italy, followed by service in Greek and Adriatic waters. She returned to home waters briefly, before being transferred for Far Eastern use. The little ship returned to the UK at Christmas 1945, and was laid up at Harwich until 1953, when she was transferred on loan to the Indian Navy and renamed RIN *Gomati*. She was bought by India in 1958. RIN *Gomati* served as a training ship for many years, before going to the breakers in 1975.

FRANCONIA AND LACONIA

The Wallsend Yard were regular suppliers of ships for the Cunard Line. Following the success of the *Mauretania*, the company were contracted to build two 18,000- ton liners for the UK-Boston route. Completed in 1911, the *Franconia* and *Laconia* were built with an eye to cruising to the Mediterranean from the USA in the winter months. Each ship could carry 2,850 passengers and 450 crew, most of whom travelled in spartan conditions in the emigrant section of the ship. *Franconia*, the first of the sisters to be completed, maintained the company's trans-Atlantic schedule until being requisitioned by the government as a troopship in 1914. She brought the first contingent of Canadian troops eastwards to fight in the war. Other missions included trooping to the Dardanelles, and when on another mission she was torpedoed and sunk by the submarine *UB47* 195 miles east of Malta in October 1916. *Laconia* was requisitioned by the Admiralty in October 1914, and spent two years under the white ensign acting as an armed merchant cruiser and storeship on the South Atlantic Station. She was involved in the hunt for the German cruiser *Konigsberg*. *Laconia* was handed back to her owners in 1916, resuming duties on the Boston route. But like her sister she was to be sunk by a U-boat, in February 1917, when *U50* claimed her, 160 miles north west of the Fastnet.

ALICE

The motor yacht *Alice* was built at Wallsend during the slump of the 1920s. The little vessel was launched in November 1929, being built for Sir Richard Cooper. This 460-ton yacht had accommodation for nine passengers and five crew. She attained 12.22 knots on trials. Three days after the outbreak of World War II *Alice* was requisitioned by the Admiralty. Initially based on the Tyne on anti-submarine operations, by 1942 she had also served in Liverpool and Larne in the same role. In 1942 a compulsory purchase order was placed on her and she was converted into an accommodation ship for Combined Operations based on the Clyde. After the war she was bought by Sir Edmund Crane, who renamed her *Natalie*. She was sold several more times and was a frequent visitor to South Africa, the Mediterranean and Channel Islands. In 1966 *Natalie* was sold to a London finance house, and during this period of her career was an extra in the film *Strawman*. In 1970 she was sold to a Japanese businessman and was used by multi-national companies for corporate hospitality and exhibition charter work in Japanese waters. In 1974 *Natalie* came to her final resting place as the centre piece of a fun park at Hiroshima. A bizarre end to a splendid looking vessel.

A DEPOSED QUEEN

In the late 1950s it became apparent to the Cunard Line that the pride of the British fleet, the ageing *Queen Mary* and *Queen Elizabeth*, would have to be replaced. The two ships had served in war and peace for 20 years. Plans were put into place to build a replacement, of similar size, 80,000 tons, 900 feet long and carrying 2,250 passengers. Dubbed the 'Q3' (Queen 3), two artist's impressions of designs are pictured here.

All the prominent British shipyards were invited to tender. Only four large yards were capable of building such a complex vessel – provision would need to be made for nuclear powered engines, then regarded as the way ahead. Swan's, and their neighbours further up the Tyne, Vickers-Armstrong (Tyne) Ltd., submitted a joint tender in 1961 under the banner of Swans-Vickers Ltd. The ship would be built at Wallsend and fitted out at the Walker yard. It would be laid down in May 1962 and completed in March 1965. The cost would be £28m. However, in October 1961 Cunard cancelled the project mainly because of poor trading and the decline in sea travel. The Swans-Vickers link-up made a bid to build a smaller replacement ship but, unbelievably to some, Cunard gave the order for the *QE2* to John Brown's yard on Clydebank.